Creating Heaven
on Planet Earth

Nondis "Angel Love" Chesnut

BALBOA.
PRESS
A DIVISION OF HAY HOUSE

A warm thank you goes to the entire Balboa Press team who made this book possible. Also, a special thank you goes to Madison Lux and Staci K. Kern who went the extra mile to achieve perfection in the production of this screenplay.

Thank you to Speedway Photo, Daytona Beach, Florida, because they made the clouds possible for the Balboa Design Team who added images and visualization to produce the magnificent cover of this book.

Balboa Press books may be ordered through booksellers or by contacting:

Balboa Press
A Division of Hay House
1663 Liberty Drive
Bloomington, IN 47403
www.balboapress.com
1-(877) 407-4847

Because of the dynamic nature of the Internet, any web addresses or links contained in this book may have changed since publication and may no longer be valid. The views expressed in this work are solely those of the author and do not necessarily reflect the views of the publisher, and the publisher hereby disclaims any responsibility for them.

ISBN: 978-1-4525-4606-3 (sc)
ISBN: 978-1-4525-4605-6 (e)

Printed in the United States of America
Balboa Press rev. date: 3/9/2012

In Memory Of

All the creators of love
and joy
who remain in our hearts

Dedicated to

Readers who are ready to heal
and wish to discover
peace, love, and joy...
You will find
your soul's purpose and
become a Creator
of Heaven on Planet Earth...
If you are holding this book,
in your hands, it is
dedicated to you.

Table of Contents

Prologue

"Love has nothing to do with what
you are expecting to get. It's what
you are expected to give."
Anonymous

This quote seems appropriate to address the readers of this book because as you enjoy the messages between these pages, you, too, will understand how you have been given given talents that God expects you to use every single day.

For me, 2011 was a year of constant surprise. A strange heavenly situation prompted me to reconsider my fate. Whenever I drove into the Daytona State College Parking Lot, December 14, 2011, every parking space seemed to be filled, except one that was waiting just for me.

After parking my car, I opened the car door and walked around to the trunk. After opening it, I paused to gaze at the sky because I was trying to determine whether I needed an umbrella, a rain coat, or nothing at all. Just then, right before my eyes, a man emerged out of the thin air. He was approximately 5'4" tall, had blonde hair, wore a white tee shirt, covered by a front opened brown sweater without buttons, and a long khaki scarf was tied around his neck. This man sported khaki shorts, white knee high socks, and brown laced shoes. Stepping back two feet, he said, "Do not be afraid. Please do not be afraid. I have a message to give to you or something to tell you, and I don't want you to fear me. I bear you no harm. I have something to tell you, but I just don't know how."

"Just spit it out," I advised. After all, what could be more surprising than seeing a man emerge from thin air?

"Just spit it out," he muttered, "okay." He paused, "I am homeless. I traveled all night on a beam just to get here. I talked to one other person at the First Baptist Church in Daytona this morning before I saw you. He told me about a homeless shelter in Deland that charges $10 for the night. The church had a Treasurer Box for people like me, but since it was so early in the morning, it was locked. But the man that I talked to gave me the seven dollars from his pocket. He said that was all he had. Do you know about the homeless shelter in Deland?"

"No," I said, "Catholic Charities is on White Street."

"Where's that?"

"It's to my right. White Street joins the college, and the Catholic Charities are located right there, so it isn't far away."

"I didn't know there was one. Thank you for telling me. But I won't need them. I just need to get to the shelter in Deland."

Thinking for a moment, I replied, "I don't know where that is."

He laughs, "I don't need directions. I'll set my beam, and it'll take me there. You could pick up your cell phone and call the police because what I am doing is known as panhandling. It's against the law, and the police could put me in jail, but somehow, I trust you. I have the seven dollars the man from the Baptist Church gave me, so I need three more dollars because he said it cost ten dollars to stay over night. It wouldn't hurt to have a couple more dollars because I'm on foot. I mean for food. I haven't eaten, and I don't know the shelter might charge a couple dollars for breakfast or the price might have gone up a couple dollars. If you could spare five dollars, I'd much appreciate it."

"If I have five dollars, I'll certainly give it to you." Looking in my billfold, I discovered a one dollar bill, a five dollar bill, and a ten dollar bill. Thinking, I wondered if I should give him the ten, but since he asked for the five, I thought that he knew I never had three dollars, and he asked me for five dollars, so I handed him the five dollars.

The gentleman bowed once, bowed the second time, did a courtesy, and said, "Thank you. God bless you. God bless you. May God bless you," and he disappeared into thin air right before my eyes.

What did his appearance mean? Certainly, his visitation was unusual. Then, again, 2011, was totally surprising because seeing Rome, Italy, Lourdes, France, and Paris, France, became a reality. Touring places that Jesus and Mary, too, had walked seemed like miracles. Witnessing and hearing about Masterpieces that men and women constructed with their own hands that lasted throughout the years made me wonder if they realized what was real at that time, undoubtedly, was not as important to them as the significances that they contributed to our future. Yes, the incredible continued whenever our group was granted an audience with The Pope, and we saw Pope Benedict as well as Pope John Paul who lay in his glass casket.

Visiting Lourdes where Mary appeared to Bernadette, and arriving weekly, thousands of people expected to be healed by the waters that sprang up where Mary promised. Also, in France, we toured Paris and visited the Louve Museum all day. Wow! We looked into the eyes of the original Mona Lisa painting.

During the summer, my husband and I were blessed with seeing the Cherokee Indian play, Oconaluftee Indian Village, the Cherokee museum, and the Biltmore in North Carolina. On the same vacation, we experienced two family reunions.

Whenever James Newport called from Balboa Press, I was thinking about these experiences and wondering what manuscript would mean the most to my readers. All signs pointed to the screenplay, *HEAVEN ON PLANET EARTH* because I thought that other screenwriters, writers, artists, and even ordinary people could create a better world. If, for example, people realized that their words, thoughts, and behavior could make a better place for individuals who experienced hurt, pain, and pure Hell, I believed within my heart that we could make a difference. God gave each of us talents that called for action, yet, too, many of us get caught up by the moment and participate in negative behaviors without realizing the consequences.

Our reality becomes watching television and hearing how the Democrats and Republicans plan to solve problems or create more conflicts. We are guilty of sitting back and watching the negatives rather than discovering the positives that God has created for us in this world.

Where is the magic? We are ready to heal, and we want happiness in our lives. Yes, each one of us has the imagination to let go and experience nature to the fullest. Certainly, we forgive and practice unconditional love. We need to surround ourselves with people who really make us feel like we are the angels on earth.

We accept the challenges that lie before us and rather than ignoring the miracles of day to day living, we must learn to pay attention to the signs of what we see before our eyes. Only then, we shall be able to change the bad into good and the negatives into positives that can create Heaven on Planet Earth.

Introduction

This script is like nothing you have ever experienced. These interactions are seeds that will produce beautiful flowers when you sow them into your daily life. Your reward will be happiness.

1. Don't let others influence your life in negative ways.

2. Let others know how much you mean to them. Check on your relatives and friends often.

3. Carefully choose words to show unconditional love.

4. Pay attention to you internal or intuitive voice.

5. There is nothing wrong with loving someone whether you are eight or eighty.

6. Loving someone is good.

7. Faulty thinking can harm, so talk about what is bugging you with a friend.

8. We should always expect a miracle.

9. Even a flower, some candy, or a pair of socks to warm one's feet can give us hope.

10. We need to pay close attention to the little things.

11. A card is most important and can be comforting.

12. Forgiving another person for causing pain is necessary.

13. We need to become one with nature.

14. Indians understood Spirit and knew life was eternal.

15. Every soul has a purpose…to find love and to give love.

16. God can help with our needs.

17. The Angels of God can be called upon to help us.

18. We have to be humble.

19. We need to be able to understand the handicapped.

20. Understanding that without love, destruction prevails is necessary to our well-being.

21. Water, air, sun, and earth are important to our Spirits.

22. Spirit can heal.

23. Eating a meal with another race helps us in our understanding.

24. We are equal in the eyes of God.

25. We must teach each other about God's Spirit.

26. Even rocks have masculine and feminine energy, known as Vortexes, and this energy is not only measurable, it can be felt by humans.

27. We are energy forces.

28. All people have been given gifts from God that are different talents than others have.

29. Love and healing are more important than sex and violence.

30. Everybody is somebody in God's eyes.

FADE IN:

HIGH OVER - CLOUDS DAY

We float above the white billowy clouds. Sky blue is the only thing between us and them. As they part we see

MATCH TO:

colorful dancing lights.

EXT - DANCING LIGHTS - EVENING

CLOSE UP, <u>SFX</u>: VCR: Dancing lights film shots with camcorder appear on the screen. (These lights are made with water and come from a huge fountain.)

<u>SOUND OF</u>: original music *"Christian Light Rock Beat"*

> to original verses, *Listen to God*
> V.O. MUSIC VOICE
> (Singing)

IF YOU'RE A TEACHER WHO WRITES IN CHALK,
MAYBE YOU DON'T BELIEVE GOD CAN TALK;
SOMEDAY HE'S GOIN' CALL ON YOU,
AND GIVE YOU A JOB TO DO.

WHEN THE LIGHT APPEARS FROM ABOVE,
THERE MAY BE MORE THERE THAN A DOVE;
LISTEN TO THE VOICE; YOU MUST OBEY,
FOR NO ONE SHOULD TELL GOD TO GO AWAY.
YOU GOTTA TAKE TIME TO LISTEN,
BY SPREADIN' HIS LOVE, PEOPLE WILL GLISTEN,
WHAT GOD HAS TO SAY IS FAR MORE IMPORTANT,
THAN MAKIN' MONEY AND SAYIN' I CAN'T.
WHEN THE LIGHT APPEARS FROM ABOVE,

THERE MAY BE MORE THERE THAN A DOVE;
LISTEN TO THE VOICE; YOU MUST OBEY,
FOR NO ONE SHOULD TELL GOD TO GO AWAY.

TIME DISSOLVE
MUSIC (CONT'D)

INT – MIDDLE SCHOOL – DAY
CHRISTIAN LIGHT ROCK MUSIC (CONT'D)
WORDS DISSOLVE; MUSIC BEAT CONT'D

MONTAGE

1) INT - DOLLY'S CLASSROOM - (2011)- DAY

The CAMERA MOVES ACROSS the English classroom, identified easily by posters. DOLLY DAY, 40, a dedicated teacher is shown. The CAMERA PASSES over the faces of MULTICULTURAL EIGHTH GRADERS. Some pupils are reading while others are writing. KAITLYN, 13, ALLISON, 12, NICOLAS, 14, and BRETT, 13, raise their hands.

CHRISTIAN LIGHT ROCK MUSIC (CONT'D)

2) INT - NICOLE'S CLASSROOM - (2011)- DAY

NICOLE PHILIPS, 30'S, a short, heavy set lady is selling hard candy to ALEXIS, 13, ROBERT, 12, AMANDA, 14, AND JASON, 13.

CAMERA MOVES to close up of Alexis paying for candy. HOLD on Alexis and Nicole Philips. CAMERA MOVES to Robert, an arrogant boy, purchasing the product. CAMERA CLOSES IN on Amanda, buying candy from Nicole Philips. HOLD ON a TIGHT SHOT OF Nicole Philips and Jason.

CAMERA PULLS BACK and MOVES AROUND the class, showing students out of their seats.

CHRISTIAN LIGHT ROCK MUSIC (CONT'D)

3) INT - DOLLY'S CLASSROOM – DAY

CAMERA MOVES around the class. Students are seated in pairs, chatting about today's lesson, even though no talking is heard.

The CAMERA MOVES IN for a TIGHT on DOLLY who is smiling. HOLD ON students, leaving one row at a time and very mannerly.

CHRISTIAN LIGHT ROCK MUSIC (CONT'D)

4) INT - SCHOOL HALLWAY - DAY

CAMERA FOCUSES IN THE HALL where students are jammed, opening lockers, throwing in books, and leaving with only candy in the palm. CLOSE IN, Jason throws a piece of candy.

SXF: INSERT: Candy whizzing through the air.

BACK ON SCENE:

MATCH TO:

Amanda dodges the candy, sailing by her right eye.

HOLD ON, Jason runs

MATCH TO:

into DOLLY's classroom.

INT - DOLLY'S CLASSROOM - DAY

Jason passes the first row of seats, rounds the corner of the second row, jumps into the air, and falls down. Struggling to get up, pains of emotions show across the face.

CAMERA CLOSES IN on DOLLY who walks to the intercom and pushes a button. PULL BACK to show Jason lying on the floor in pain.

CHRISTIAN LIGHT ROCK MUSIC (CONT'D)

6) EXT - SCHOOL SIDE WALK - DAY

CAMERA MOVES to students leaving the building for home. HOLD ON, Alexis who in turn bumps Robert who thinks Amanda pushed him. CLOSE IN, Alexis turns and runs toward the building from which she came. CLOSE UP of Amanda pointing finger at Alexis. PULL BACK as Robert looks toward Alexis and gives Alexis his hand. She gets up limping.

CHRISTIAN LIGHT ROCK MUSIC (CONT'D)

7) EXT - SCHOOL GROUND, MEDICAL CENTER - DAY

HOLD ON the swollen knot on the corner of Alexis' eye. PULL BACK to show her looking at the sign. CLOSE UP of words MEDICAL CENTER CLOSED FOR THE DAY.

CAMERA MOVES to Amanda. FOCUS ON her sprained ankle and bloody knee. PULL BACK to DOLLY Day, who is pushing Jason in the wheel chair toward the girls and the Medical Center.

CHRISTIAN LIGHT ROCK MUSIC (CONT'D)
THROUGH TO

8) INT - VICE PRINCIPAL'S OFFICE - DAY

DOLLY talks to KATHERINE, 25, a secretary wearing glasses, sits at a desk. Alexis and Amanda are seated in straight back chairs. Jason is in the wheelchair. Katherine isn't able to help DOLLY with any ice and doesn't have any container for it. DOLLY persists. Perhaps Katherine has a rubber glove. CLOSE IN as Katherine pulls two rubber gloves from a file cabinet and hands them to DOLLY. HOLD ON a CUSTODIAN, 27, entering the office. PULL BACK to show DOLLY receiving the gloves. The CAMERA MOVES IN as the custodian walks toward the door and leaves the office.

MONTAGE ENDS

MUSIC DISSOLVES
DISSOLVE TO:

INT - VICE PRINCIPAL'S OFFICE - DAY

Jason is in the wheelchair, looking like he's in pain. Alexis and Amanda are seated talking to Jason. DOLLY calls the parents, and the custodian returns with the ice.

The CAMERA MOVES IN on DOLLY Day who begins dialing the phone.

>   DOLLY
>   (Into phone)
> This is Ms. Day. Jason is sitting here
> beside me. We need you to come pick him
> up. Don't get alarmed, but he may need to
> go to the doctor. Jason slipped in my room.
> His foot may be sprained or broken.

CAMERA MOVES to the Custodian who returns with the ice in two gloves. DOLLY hands one to Alexis.

>   ALEXIS
>   (With sincerity)
> My mom should be here soon. Thanks for
> calling her. I do hope this ice will help.
> I hate going to the doctor.

CLOSE UP, DOLLY hands the glove filled with ice to Amanda.

>   AMANDA
>   (Deep in thought)
> I can't get over it. The nurse left.
> The vice principal went home.
> The secretary refused help. And you offered
> to help us, Ms. Day.

> DOLLY
> (Smiling)
>> I couldn't have done anything without
>> Tim, our custodian.

CAMERA PANS to the Custodian's smiling face that seems to be glowing in appreciation. LONG SHOT of DOLLY and students.

> DOLLY
> (Confidently)
>> Your parents should be arriving soon.
>> I phoned all of them.

MONTAGES END

> MUSIC ENDS

INT - CLASSROOM - DAY

The CAMERA MOVES IN as DOLLY sits at the desk alone. She moves to the computer.

SXF: A LIGHT COMES AND SOFTENS, as it shines on DOLLY's body.

HOLD ON COMPUTER SCREEN. FOCUS on words. SFX: White light appears and shines rays on DOLLY.

BACK ON SCENE

CLOSE UP of the computer screen.

> COMPUTER SCREEN
>> You must become a screenwriter.
>> You must work for God.

SFX: White light, an amorphous form, enters the room.

CLOSE UP of the white light, representing God's voice.

GOD'S VOICE V.O.
(Hollow Echoing Whisper)
Leave. Get in your car.

GOD'S VOICE V.O. (CONT'D)
I'll guide you. Follow me.

PULL BACK to DOLLY.

DOLLY
(Mortified)
God, I'm frightened. You don't mean me.
I can't do this!

EXT - DOLLY'S CAR - TRAVEL SHOT - DAY
CAMERA SHOT of a car in motion.
INT - DOLLY'S CAR - TRAVEL SHOT - DAY

DOLLY
(Baffled)
Is there anybody there?

SFX: White light, representing God, can be seen in the car.

GOD'S VOICE V.O.
(Filtered)
(Hollow Echoing Whisper)
Yes. I'm here.

PULL BACK to show DOLLY and the light.

DOLLY
(Fearful)
What do you want from me?
Are you from the devil or from God?

SXF: White light moves in the car.

CLOSE UP: White light

> GOD'S VOICE V.O.
> (Filtered)
> (Calculated)
> I am your supreme being. I'll guide you.
> Turn here.

> DOLLY
> (Angry)
> I wish you would just go away. Leave me alone!

> GOD'S VOICE V.O.
> (Firmly)
> I'm not going anywhere. You have been chosen.

EXT – RESTAURANT – Day

(Optional: This scene may be shot on location at the *LOST IN TIME RESTAURANT*, Cassadaga, Florida.)

The CAMERA RIDES on DOLLY who parks the car in front of the *Lost in Time Restaurant*. She walks across the street and goes into the bookstore.

INT - BOOKSTORE- DAY

(Optional: This scene may be shot on location at the bookstore in Cassadaga, Florida.)

HOLD ON a clerk, SARAH, 40's, is behind the cash registrar.

PULL BACK to show CUSTOMER ONE, 25, a tall, red head, and

CUSTOMER TWO, 35, a short, brunette, medium build, comes into the bookstore where DOLLY observes.

The CAMERA MOVES around the bookstore showing some of the titles of books with a CLOSE UP, *The Path to Love, Spirit Whisperer, Commune with the Angels, You Can Create An Exceptional Life, A Touch of Love from Heaven, Healing Words, Deep Truth, Through Time Into Healing, Change your Thoughts – Change your Life.*

BACK ON SCENE:

CAMERA MOVES IN on Sarah and DOLLY.

> SARAH
> (To DOLLY)
>
> Watch!

CAMERA MOVES to the two customers who enter the bookstore.

CLOSE UP, <u>SFX</u>: as name and address cards fly off the wall, drop to the floor, one flies back up into Customer One's hands.

BACK ON SCENE:

PULL BACK to show all four women: Customer One, Customer Two, DOLLY, and Sarah. CAMERA MOVES IN on the three women:

Customer One, Sarah, and Customer Two. CAMERA MOVES CLOSER to show only Sarah and Customer One.

> CUSTOMER ONE
> (Demanding)
>
> I must see this person. She has a sunflower
> in the garden.

> SARAH
> (Very stern)
>
> All the readers' appointments are filled.
> You need an appointment.

CUSTOMER ONE
(Assured and insistent)
This card came to me. This woman has a
sunflower in her garden. I've driven
thousands of miles to see her.
(Repeats)

CUSTOMER ONE (CONT'D)
She has a sunflower in the garden.

CAMERA PULLS BACK to show Customer Two also.

CUSTOMER TWO
(Meekly)
I came with her. I want to go too.

SARAH
(Cautiously)
I'll phone her and see.

CLOSE UP, Sarah picks up the phone and dials.

SARAH (CONT'D)
(Into the phone)
I have a customer here who wants a reading.
The reason I called was your card flew
off the wall, dropped to the floor, and
then, managed to fly into her hand.
(Pause)

SARAH (CONT'D 2)
Yes, she knows you have a sunflower in
the garden. This woman claims she drove
thousands of miles to see you.
(Pause)

SARAH (CONT'D 3)

Just a minute.

(Pause)

SARAH (CONT'D 4)

(To Customer One)

How do you know there's a sunflower in her garden?

CUSTOMER ONE

(Pleading)

I had a dream. Tell her I must see her.
Explain I know she has red hair.

SARAH

(Into the phone)

She says she had a dream, and she must see
you. She just told me your hair is red.

(Pauses; listening)

SARAH (CONT'D)

Okay. That will make her happy. Bye.

(Sarah hangs up the phone and looks at Customer One.)

SARAH (CONT'D 2)

(Sternly)

She'll see you now but not your friend.

PULL BACK to show the disappointment in Customer Two's face.

CUSTOMER TWO

(Disappointed)

That hurts! I drove thousands of miles
with her.

> SARAH
>
> Sorry! Better luck next time. Appointments
> for readings need to be made in advance.

> CUSTOMER ONE
>
> Do you have the directions to her house?

> SARAH
>
> You won't need them. You'll find her the
> same way you found your way here.

CAMERA MOVES IN on both ladies leaving the store.

EXT - BOOKSTORE – DAY

Customer Two stays on the porch while Customer One walks onward, and then, makes a left hand turn on the street beside the store.

INT - BOOKSTORE – DAY

HOLD ON Sarah as she eyes DOLLY.

> SARAH
> (Assuring)
> You will find answers in the gardens.

EXT - ANGEL GARDEN – DAY

HOLD ON DOLLY who sits quietly in the garden. An angel with wings statue is in the center of the garden. Flowers and other green plants are situated in this peaceful setting.

(Optional: This Angel Garden can be found on site beside the bookstore in Cassadaga, Florida.)

FADE IN, <u>SXF</u>: SOFTEN LIGHTS, FOUR ANGELS appear...
MICHAEL in a blue robe, RAPHAEL in a pink robe, GABRIEL in a
white robe, and URIEL, in a ruby robe.

<u>SXF</u>: An aura shines around each angel's body and head in the color
matching the attire.

<u>SFX</u>: A White Light appears over the angels' heads, and God's voice is
heard.

CLOSE UP on the White Light.

> GOD'S VOICE V.O.
> (Hollowing echoing deep-throated)
> You must help the angels. You will bring
> the people to understand God and His love.

MOVE TO the angels. CLOSE UP of DOLLY.

> DOLLY
> (Mystified)
> I hate being an antagonist, but I don't know
> how. Why don't you ask someone else who
> understands these things? Like a minister?
> Maybe a Father? Okay, a Reverend would do!
> But not me!

EXT - HEALING GARDEN – DAY

HOLD ON CLOSE UP of DOLLY sitting on a bench. (Optional:
The *Healing Garden* can be found on site in Cassadaga, Florida. On the
other hand, another desired location can be utilized.)

INSERT: ZOOM IN SPACE IN WOODED AREA FROM ONE TREE TO ANOTHER ONE and into the woods...

BACK ON SCENE:

BURN IN: DOLLY is looking upward. CLOSE UP on DOLLY.

> DOLLY
> (Amazed)
> Humans are somewhat like squirrels,
> only limitless in the imagination
> of what they can do.

INSERT: STOCK SHOT, ZOOM TO CUT OF A SQUIRREL in a tree,

> or

VCR: CUT MATCHED of flying squirrels in the *Healing Gardens,* Cassadaga, Florida, taken with camcorder.

BACK ON DOLLY who is talking to herself out loud.

> DOLLY (CONT'D)
> (Softly)
> Now I understand why Dad used to hunt.

INSERT: CUT OF PICTURE OF PEACEFUL WOODLANDS.

BACK ON SCENE. CLOSE UP on DOLLY, talking to herself.

> DOLLY (CONT'D) 2
> (Deep in thought)
> What a beautiful sight! If people dare
> to dream, then nature can heal.
> If we dare to give unselfish love,
> then anything is possible.

The sound of mysterious soft music begins.

MYSTERIOUS MUSIC

The CAMERA FOLLOWS DOLLY into a path into the woods.

INSERT: CUT TO a picture of thick woods.

BACK ON SCENE: HOLD ON DOLLY and ZOOM IN on her eyes.

INSERT: STOCK SHOT, a picture of a blue jay and other birds.

BACK ON SCENE: The CAMERA ZOOMS to DOLLY who is now shown in confusion and bewilderment.

INSERT: STOCK CUT, picture of burned ashes on the ground.

MUSIC DISSOLVES

BACK ON SCENE: CLOSE ON DOLLY...

DOLLY (CONT'D) 3
(Looking down nervously)

I smell ashes! I smell ashes!

The sound of mysterious soft music picks up tempo, and develops into the sounds of Indian warriors going into battle.

MYSTERIOUS MUSIC (CONT'D)
THROUGH TO:

INSERT: CUTS OF INDIAN PICTURES FADE IN.

MUSIC (CONT'D)

EXT - COUNTRY WOODED AREA - DAY

INSERT: VCR CLOSE UP STOCK CUT: as far as the eye can see, Indians, four, five abreast, and the Chief on Horseback, coming toward the CAMERA with bows and arrows...

DISSOLVE TO:

BACK ON SCENE: DOLLY runs from the Indian site.

MUSIC DISSOLVES TO:

CLOSE UP on DOLLY...

> DOLLY
> (Exasperated)
> I get the message I think. Don't hurt me!

EXT - PARK - CASSADAGA, FLORIDA - DAY

DISTANCE ANGLE OF ENTIRE SCENE: Green grass is seen. A lake borders the grass. On the other side of the water is a lone, antiquated, house that looks desolate. At the bottom of the hill is a gazebo. DOLLY sits at a white bench when she hears an ELDERLY WOMAN'S VOICE speaking. The voice seems to come <u>SXF</u>: from a green light about the size of a watermelon appears. BACK ON SCENE, CAMERA CLOSE UP of the light. PULL BACK to get a visual of DOLLY and the light. CAMERA MOVES IN on DOLLY.

> ELDERLY WOMAN'S VOICE V.O.
> (Filtered)
> (Comes from the green light)
> I lived on the earth for a hundred years.
> Now I'm on the other side.

BACK TO DOLLY.

DOLLY
(Unbelievingly)
Are you talking to me?

BACK TO green light.

ELDERLY WOMAN'S VOICE
(Firmly)
DOLLY, you need to tell people about love.

PULL BACK to DOLLY and the green light.

DOLLY
(Nervous, trying to remain calm)
Why me? You're scaring me. Go away.

CAMERA FOLLOWS as DOLLY gets up, turns away, and walks toward the gazebo.

INSERT (OPTION 1): Cut to picture of a SQUIRREL in a tree.

INSERT CUT close up of a squirrel on a limb.

INSERT (OPTION 2): VCR of a SQUIRREL in a tree.

INSERT (OPTION 3): Shot on location at *Healing Gardens*, Cassadaga, Florida, of SQUIRRELS.

INSERT (OPTION 4): Shot on location, Brevard Zoo, 8225 N. Wickham Road, Melbourne, Florida, SQUIRRELS, and other animals, such as, a fawn deer, a white tail deer, a bald eagle, and a barred owl are photographed.

BACK ON DOLLY, take a camera shot moving from her waist upward, prior to MOVING IN on the face, and then, INSERT CLOSE-UP of her eyeballs, as the eyes open wide in surprise.

> DOLLY
> (Surprised; amazement on the face)
> What are you saying?

INSERT: CAMERA RETURNS TO CUT of the squirrel, and the sound of the squirrel's voice is heard. (OPTIONAL: the director may choose another animal in place of the squirrel if desired).

> SQUIRREL'S VOICE V.O.
> (Filtered)
> (Eerie, phantom, squeaky voice)
> You must help the children.

BACK ON SCENE. CLOSE UP of DOLLY who is looking upward at the animal.

> DOLLY
> (Innocently)
> Me? How? I don't understand.

CAMERA FOLLOWS as DOLLY walks away.

EXT -FIELD/ LAKE HELEN, CASSADAGA, FLORIDA, HOUSE SCENE –DAY

WIDE ANGLE SHOT of the house across the lake. CAMERA ZOOMS SLOWLY on a closer shot of the old, antiquated, deserted looking, gray house that can be seen from across the lake.

CAMERA MOVES IN for a closer shot of the house. The sound of a baby's cry, followed by a child's scream is heard by DOLLY.

She tries to move away from the anguish. Since she doesn't know what to do, she walks into the woods where she sees a BIRD on a stump, a DEER, BUTTERFLIES, a WHITE DOVE, and SWANS.

BABY'S CRY V.O.
(Sound of a baby cry)
INSERT: STOCK sound of a baby crying.
Eeeeeeeeeee! Eeeeeeeee! Eeeeeeeeeeee!

CHILD'S SCREAM V.O.
(High pitched)
Heeeeelllppp meeee! Heeeeelllppp meeee!

HOLD ON DOLLY who turns and looks toward the house in bewilderment.

CHILD'S SCREAM V.O. CONT'D)
Heeeeelllppp meeee! Heeeeelllppp meeee!

CAMERA FOLLOWS DOLLY who walks up another path and into the woods. A <u>sound of rustling leaves can be heard. Add sounds of a wild turkey.</u> INSERT CLOSE UP of a turkey.

QUICKCUTS (option one)

1)   INSERT CUT of pictures of butterflies.

2)   INSERT CUT of a photo of a duck.

3)   INSERT CUT of a photo of a turtle.

FILM ON LOCATION (option two)

CAMERA SHOT of American alligator, American crocodiles, North America bobcat, wild turkey, a red fox, and a Bald Eagle which is captured on film at the Brevard Zoo, Melbourne, Florida.

ADD ADDITIONAL INTEREST by shooting film of the endangered species of manatees playing, shot on location from the Manatee Viewing Area off the bridge at the National Wildlife Reserve in Brevard County,

Florida. Moths, butterflies, and birds are plentiful here, and captured on film as well.

BACK ON SCENE. HOLD ON DOLLY, looking to the right… She sees the lake, and the house in the distance.

ANGLE SHOT of the lake in the distance.

COMPUTER SHOT (Option 1) of a WHITE DOVE flying upward in the sky.

VCR STOCK SHOT (Options 2) of a WHITE DOVE flying upward in the sky.

FILMED ON LOCATION at the Brevard Zoo, Melbourne, FL, (Option 3) of a white bird flying upward.

BACK ON SCENE. DOLLY sits down on a stump. INSERT: SHOCK SHOT of woods in the background or film on scene in Cassadaga, Florida. CAMERA MOVES IN on DOLLY's head.

INSERT: CUT TO of the photo of the brain. <u>SXF</u>: Soft multicolor lights flash and cover the whole screen.

TIME DISSOLVE

FLASHBACK

<u>SXF</u>: Neon lights flash the numbers 1997.

MATCH TO:

INT - BEDROOM - (1997) - NIGHT

"HARP MUSIC" Begins

DOLLY lies in bed. VIRGIN MARY appears in a white robe with a blue sash tied around her waist. DOLLY turns in bed. HOLD ON DOLLY's body from the waist up. MOVE TO DOLLY's face and show her opening her eyes in surprise. She shuts them in disbelief, and opens them again. MOVE TO the Virgin Mary.

<u>SXF</u>: Surround the Virgin Mary with a mixture of white and blue lights, forming an aura over her entire body. BACK ON SCENE: The Virgin Mary stands at the foot of the bed. Even though she does not move her lips, Virgin Mary's voice is heard.

MUSIC DISSOLVES
THROUGH TO:

VIRGIN MARY V.O.
(Filtered; soft whisper)
Help/allow the children to come unto me.

DOLLY
(Dazed)
I don't understand. Help? Allow? What?
I must be dreaming.

VIRGIN MARY V.O
(Filtered; soft whisper)
You're awake. I'm really here.
Help allow the children to come unto me.

<u>SFX</u>: Virgin Mary vanishes right before DOLLY's eyes.

BACK ON SCENE. CLOSE UP of DOLLY's dazed reaction.

END FLASHBACK

<u>SFX</u>: Multicolor soft colors swirl on the total screen.

MATCH TO
<u>SFX</u>: Neon lights show the year 2011.

BACK ON SCENE. CAMERA MOVES IN on DOLLY as she sits in the woods.

DOLLY
(Talking out loud to herself)
What is the purpose of the dove? (Pause)
Is this a sign of love, peace, or the Holy
Spirit?(Pause)
Why is there a child crying for help? (Pause)
Is there a connection between that child's cry
and the Virgin Mary appearing to me in my
bedroom?
(Pause)
What do you expect me to do, God?

SFX: An amorphous phantom of a huge white image appears in sky. BACK
ON SCENE. HOLD ON DOLLY looking up at the white image, but
there is only silence. DOLLY shakes her head, "No".
HARP MUSIC begins

EXT - WOODS, MEADOW, ROAD, YARD WITH A HOUSE -
DAY
CAMERA RIDES on DOLLY who leaves the path in the wooded area
MATCH CUT TO
and returns to the meadow,
MATCH CUT TO
walks up the hill
MATCH CUT TO

and continues down a hard road surface. She sees a sign in the front yard
and walks toward it. INSERT: CUT TO words on the sign "Reverend".
BACK ON SCENE: CAMERA RIDES on DOLLY who walks toward
the sign and the house located behind it, but she changes her mind, backs
up, and continues on the road.

INSERT: CUT TO clip of the sun. SFX: Rays come from the sun.

A powerful white light fills up the screen, and then, moves to one side and streams downward as DOLLY watches.

BURN IN: CLOSE UP - DOLLY looks heavenward toward the sun, and the rays coming from it.

> *HARP MUSIC* DISSOLVES
> THROUGH TO:
>
> DOLLY
> (Exasperated)

What do you want from me, God?
What is my soul's purpose?
How can I obey when I'm not sure how?
Okay, if I could write what you want me, too?
There is no market for your work.
How can I get a director sold on the idea
of putting God on the screen?
Why don't you go and get yourself
a well-known screenwriter or a famous director?
Why are you always picking on me?
I'm just a nobody.

DISSOLVE TO
EXT - LOST IN TIME RESTAURANT - DAY

A shot of any restaurant as DOLLY enters. On the other hand, shot on location, the LOST IN TIME RESTAURANT, Cassadaga, Florida, would be great for this scene.

DISSOLVE TO
INT - LOST IN TIME RESTAURANT - DAY

Victorian curtains, pink table cloths, pink carnation center pieces, and even pictures on the walls combine pink and pastel colors, creating a stress free atmosphere.

DOLLY looks at the pamphlet lying on the table, and CASEY, 25, wearing a pink and green pastel dress approaches and hands her a menu. Casey leaves, and DOLLY begins having flashbacks.

In the first series of FLASHBACKS, JUSTIN, 53, is at the funeral home surrounded by his SIX ADULT CHILDREN plus DOLLY and THOMAS, 17, a high school senior. In the casket lies his WIFE. A series of events take place, causing Justin and Thomas to join SHELDON, DOLLY's husband, and LAUREN, her high school daughter in their home. Thomas meets another TEEN at the bus stop and there's a DRIVER of the bus. Through new opportunities, Justin and Thomas buy a new home. Then, after his retirement party with his COWORKERS, Justin meets TERA, who becomes his wife, and her FIVE CHILDREN join them at the wedding ceremony.

DOLLY returns to the present and orders from the menu.

FLASHBACKS

SXF: Multicolor, soft pastel shades swirl on the total screen. BACK ON SCENE. CLOSE UP - CALENDAR pages turn rapidly backward. CLOSE UP of the words "December, 2005."

MONTAGE(S)

FUNERAL MUSIC BEGINS

1) INT - FUNERAL HOME - DECEMBER, 2005 - NIGHT

DOLLY walks over to the casket where her MOTHER, 50, lies wearing a blue dress. Her brown, shoulder length hair is pulled back. DOLLY moves closer to her Mother's face, and she cries.

JUSTIN, 53, her father, brunette hair shows gray streaks, comes in with tears in his eyes and hugs DOLLY. They cry together. CUTS OF FOUR OTHER ADULT CHILDREN are shown. One teenage son, THOMAS,

17, is standing at the casket. His brothers and sisters are surrounding the casket.

"MUSIC" CHANGES
TIME DISSOLVE

CLOSE UP, CALENDAR reads "December, 2006".

"SAD MUSIC" BEGINS

2) EXT - SMALL TOWN AIRPLANE FACTORY – December 2006 – DAY

The Airplane Factory is shown. A sign reads "Closed" and is placed over the door. Justin walks away with tears in his eyes

MATCH CUT TO

and walks home. CAMERA MOVES to a small four room home with a porch and bath.

TIME DISSOLVE

CLOSE UP, CALENDAR reads June 2006.

"MUSIC ENDS"
DISSOLVE TO

3) EXT - JUSTIN'S HOME - NIGHT

Sounds of thunder and down pouring rain are heard.. SFX: Lightening flashes everywhere. VCR: STOCK SHOT CLIP of a hurricane destroying Justin's home.

MATCH TO

4) INT - JUSTIN'S CAR- TRAVEL SHOT - CITY - NIGHT

The sound of eerie music is heard coming from their radio.

Justin is seated beside Thomas, 17, his son, who is seen driving at night while rain and thunder pour on the windows outside the car.

"MUSIC CHANGES"
MATCH TO
"PEACEFUL MUSIC"

5) INT- DOLLY'S HOME - DAY

Justin and Thomas are shown with DOLLY, SHELDON, her husband, LAUREN, 18, a high school age daughter. They are eating at the kitchen table. DOLLY gets up, answers the door, and Sheldon and Lauren join her, as Justin and Thomas enter. They hug one another, and Justin goes with Thomas who carries their suitcases into a bedroom.

TIME DISSOLVE

CLOSE UP, CALENDAR reads "July, 2006"

"MUSIC CONTINUED"

6) EXT - ANY CITY – Airplane Factory- DAY

Justin is shown going to work with lunch box and enters the Airport Factory.

TIME DISSOLVE

CLOSE UP, CALENDAR reads "September, 2006"

"MUSIC CONTINUED"

7) EXT - BUS STOP - DAY

Thomas carries a notebook, meets another HIGH SCHOOL MALE TEENAGER, and they get on the school bus. No one else is on the bus except for the DRIVER.

"MUSIC CHANGES"
TIME DISSOLVE
"HAPPY MUSIC"

CLOSE UP OF CALENDAR, "October, 2006"

8) EXT - JUSTIN'S NEW HOME - DAY

Justin and Thomas are shown with their suitcases. A furniture van arrives and a living room sofa is carried into the two stories older home that has a front porch where Justin and Thomas are seen.

"MUSIC CHANGES"
"TIME DISSOLVE"

CLOSE UP OF CALENDAR, "June, 2009"
                  "GRADUATION MARCH"
                  MUSIC
12- INT - SCHOOL - NIGHT
Thomas is shown graduating in a cap and gown.
                  "MUSIC CHANGES"
                  TIME DISSOVE
CLOSE UP: "June 2009"
                  "PARTY MUSIC"
13) INT- RETIREMENT PARTY -NIGHT

Justin is shown at a retirement party easily noted due to the balloons reading "Retiring", flying in the air.
                  "MUSIC CHANGES"
                  TIME DISSOLVE
CLOSE UP, "September, 2009"
                  "WEDDING MUSIC"
14) EXT- CHURCH - DAY

Justin is shown with his new bride TERA, a slim, gray haired lady, who laughs easily. SIX ADULT CHILDREN, four women and two men, are on one side of the church door, and DOLLY is one of them. Tera's FIVE ADULT CHILDREN stand on the other side near their mother. All of them throw rice on Justin and Tera, as they leave the church after their wedding.
                  "MUSIC DISSOLVES"

MONTAGES END

END FLASHBACK

SFX: Multicolor soft colors swirl on the total screen.

BACK ON SCENE.

CLOSE UP OF CALENDAR, PRESENT, "2011"

CASEY
(Enthusiastic)
May I take your order now?

DOLLY
(Warmly)
A salad and a soda of some kind.
That will be all.

CASEY
(Still enthusiastic)
Which salad? And what kind of soda?

DOLLY
(Politely)
You choose. Today seems like one where I have choice. If you choose, maybe, I'll understand the solutions to my problems.

Casey writes something on a pad, smiles, and walks away, as if she understands completely.

INT - RESTAURANT - DAY (CONT'D)

While DOLLY is waiting for her food, she has other flashbacks of when her father and stepmother were happy dancing in each other's arms, until JOY, Tera's married daughter comes home to die with cancer. WILLIAM DOYLE, Joy's husband, comes to his wife's bedside. After Joy passes on, there is communication from the other side with DOLLY. She talks on the phone with someone from hospice to reveal these factors.

Casey returns with the food, and after the waitress leaves, DOLLY goes into another series of flashbacks beginning with her parents going to the grocery store, and afterwards, Justin getting pains in his heart, yet no one is told.

While DOLLY thinks about what must have happened, she is able to understand Tera's thoughts, and even, brings up Tera's flashbacks in which Justin, her daughters Joy, and DOT ROWLAND play a big part.

The flashbacks continue when Casey returns to find out how the salad is. DOLLY and she start developing deeper understandings.

FLASHBACK

SFX: Soft multicolor swirls cover the screen.

TIME DISSOLVE

BACK ON SCENE: CLOSE UP, CALENDAR, "November 2010"

MONTAGE

"BIG BAND MUSIC"

1) INT - BALLROOM - NIGHT

Justin and Tera dance. The sound of big band music is heard as the couple dances happily in each other's arms to the slow music.

MUSIC CONT'D

DISSOLVE THROUGH TO

TIME DISSOLVE

CLOSE UP, CALENDAR, "May 2010"

2) INT- JUSTIN AND TERA'S LIVING ROOM - DAY

Justin and Tera are sitting on the sofa. JOY, 30, shoulder length blonde hair with bands, medium build, seated adjacent to them in a chair.

JOY
(Letting Mom know a decision)

Mom, I came home to die or to get well.

I have cancer and less than six months to live.

TIME DISSOLVE

CLOSE UP, CALENDAR, "July 2010". The one is circled in red.

3) INT - BEDROOM - NIGHT

Joy is in bed dying with cancer. WILBER DOYLE, 40's, medium build, partly bald headed man, dictator type, is at his wife's bedside. When Tera enters the room, Wilber gets up off the bed and sends Mother away.

> WILBER
> (Dictating orders)
> Joy and I have been married for years.
> You go back downstairs. I'll take care of her.

> TIME DISSOLVE

CLOSE UP, CALENDAR, "July 15, 2010". The fifteenth is circled in red.

William covers Joy's face with the sheet, and picks up the phone.

> TIME DISSOLVE

5) INT - KITCHEN - DAY (10 A.M.)

DOLLY is talking on the phone. A kitchen clock points to 10:00 a.m.

> DOLLY
> (Into the phone, sternly)
> Yes, I know Joy passed to the other side last night.
> (Pause)
> She told me.(Pause)
> `DOLLY (CONT'D)
> You see, she's not really dead. Her spirit is alive.
> Joy told me herself. (Pause)
> Yes, she's here with me now. Only her body is in the
> casket.

> TIME DISSOLVE

6) INT - FUNERAL HOME - NIGHT

Joy is shown in the casket in a white dress. There are yellow roses on top the casket.

MONTAGE ENDS

FLASHBACK ENDS

SXF: Soft multicolor swirls cover the screen.

BACK ON SCENE: PULL BACK on Casey and DOLLY.

> CASEY
> You look as if you're thinkin' about the past.

> DOLLY
> Yes. How did you know?

> CASEY
> (With understanding)
> The look on your face…
> They don't call this place Endless Memories
> for nothin'.

> DOLLY
> (Wondering)
> Lots of people dream here?

CAMERA MOVES IN on Casey.

> CASEY
> (Patronizing)
> Seems that way. We don't rush people.
> Time to think seems most important here.

CLOSE UP of salad and MOVE IN on DOLLY.

> DOLLY
> (Grinning)
> That salad looks good.

PULL BACK TO Casey and DOLLY.

> CASEY
> (Responds with a grin)
> Hope ya like it! Apples with rice, raisins, lettuce,
> and other stuff with house dressing…

> DOLLY
> That's different.

> CASEY
> (Smoothly)
> Most things are here. Hope you enjoy.
> Take your time.

CAMERA MOVES in on the waitress walking off. CLOSE UP, DOLLY picks up the folk.

BACK ON SCENE, PULL BACK to show distance shot of restaurant, and DOLLY at the table.

FLASHBACK

CLOSE UP of DOLLY's head. INSERT: CUT TO photo of the brain. SXF: Multicolors flash on the screen. BACK ON SCENE: CALENDAR turns backward from 2012 to "August 29, 2010".

MONTAGE

1) INT - JUSTIN'S CAR - TRAVEL SHOT – NIGHT

2) CAMERA MOVES INTO the car. SXF: Rain pours outside the car windows; the sound of thunder is heard; and lightening flashes. BACK

ON SCENE: Groceries are in the back seat of the car. Justin and Tera are in the front seat.

2) EXT - JUSTIN'S CAR –NIGHT

3) Justin and Tera lift the groceries from an older model car.

MATCH CUT TO

They start carrying the groceries into the house. The sound of thunder is heard. <u>SFX</u>: Lightening flashes. BACK ON SCENE: HOLD ON Justin who grabs at his heart and the groceries fly everywhere. He stumbles but doesn't fall. Pain is seen across his face.

PULL BACK to show Tera continuing to carry her bag of groceries.

MATCH CUT TO

into the two story antiquated, gray house, and paying no attention to Justin's mishap.

3) INT - HOUSE - BEDROOM - NIGHT

MOVE IN on Justin who lies down on the bed and is holding his hand on his heart. MOVE TO Tera who goes to the window and tries to remove the air conditioner.

> TERA
> (Angry)
> Would you get up off the bed and help?

> JUSTIN
> (Painfully in disbelief)
> Help what? I have pains in my chest.

> TERA
> (Orders; screams)
> Pains or no pains, this thing has got to come out!
> Help me!

CLOSE UP as Tera screams, "Help me". PULL BACK to show Justin getting up and obeying. INSERT: The air conditioner hits the floor, and there is a loud sound of a bang. BACK ON SCENE: PULL BACK to show Tera and capturing Justin, falling down. He lies there without moving.

> TERA
> (Disgusted)

Get up!
(She jerks at his arm.)
> (Repeats in disgust)

Get up!

> JUSTIN
> (Pitiably)

I think I've had a heart attack!
CLOSE UP on Justin, continuing to lie there.

> TERA
> (Sarcastic)

Justin, you're over reacting. You'll be fine.
Get up!
TIME DISSOLVE

TERA'S FLASHBACK

CAMERA FOCUSES ON CLOSE-UP of Tera's head. INSERT: STOCK SHOT of brain. <u>SXF</u>: Multicolors flash on the screen.
DISSOLVE TO

<u>QUICK CUTS</u>
1) Joy is dead in the casket.

2) Justin is dead in the casket.

3) An airplane is flying.

4) Tera is seated on an airplane seat.

5) Cacti are seen.

6) Tera is shown with DOT ROLAND, 20'S, her daughter, laughing and walking in a California style home.

TERA'S FLASHBACK ENDS

<u>SFX</u>: Multicolor prisms of light flash on the screen.

BACK ON SCENE: CAMERA PANS IN on Casey.

>   CASEY
>   (Questioningly)
> How's the salad?

PULL BACK on DOLLY.

>   DOLLY
>   (Baffled)
> Huh? Oh, good. I mean delicious. Why am I lying?
> I haven't even taken the second bite. I was
> remembering.

>   CASEY
>   (Calculated)
> It must have been important.

>   DOLLY
>   (Delicately)
> Yes. It was, but I was wondering what the past
> has to do with now.

>   CASEY
>   (Enthusiastic)
> Everything. Nothin' happens by accident.
> Try the salad.

DOLLY
(Smiling)
The apples are delightful. Kind of crunchy...

CASEY
(Expectantly)
What do they remind you of?

INSERT: STOCK SHOT of Adam and Eve in words with an apple tree.
BACK ON SCENE: CLOSE UP on DOLLY.

DOLLY
(Thinking)
Eve in the *Bible* when Adam yielded to temptation.
But how does that fit into my life now?
PULL BACK on Casey.

CASEY
(Seriously)
Maybe you know somebody who sinned, and
you're thinkin' about them.

DOLLY
(Amused)
Could be.

CASEY
(Wisely)
As you eat your salad, you'll get other thoughts.

DOLLY
(Intellectually)
Like the white of this apple represents
the pure of heart.

CASEY
(Nonchalantly)
Yeah? It could be either, sin or pure.
Just like this world.

CAMERA PULLS BACK, Casey walks off. MOVE IN, DOLLY takes
another bite, and rests her hand on her chin as she remembers.

FLASHBACK

CLOSE UP of DOLLY's head. <u>INSERT</u>: photo of the brain.

<u>SFX</u>: multicolor swirls on screen. CLOSE UP on calendar

August 25, 2010. The twenty-fifth is circled in red.

"MYSTERIOUS MUSIC" BEGINS

MONTAGE

1) INT -SCHOOL LIBRARY, 2010, - Day

    a) DOLLY is feeling an underlying tension. She is explaining to
       JUNE PRICE, the librarian that something is wrong.

    b) June hands DOLLY some art books.

    c) DOLLY is seen holding the books.

    d) June gives DOLLY a book of "Renaissance Art".

MATCH TO

CAMERA MOVES IN on DOLLY's head and CUT TO photo of a
brain.

<u>SFX</u>: multicolor swirls flash on the screen.

TIME DISSOLVE

CALENDAR turns to August 2, 2010. The two is circled in red.

RENAISSANCE FLASHBACK:

MONTAGED (CONT'D)

2) Ext – RENAISSANCE FAIR, AUGUST, 2010 - DAY

An actor, dresses as Shakespeare, is writing poetry for five dollars a poem. He sends DOLLY to the Abby to copy part of a Shakespeare Sonnet.

3) EXT – ABBY- DAY

A STOCKSHOT of an Abby is needed here.

4) INT – ABBY – DAY

DOLLY looks at the NUN behind the cash registrar.

<u>SFX</u>: Two light rays go from the nun's eyes to Dolly's eyes. <u>INSERT: CUT TO</u> photo of the Mona Lisa. The nun's face is compared to the Mona Lisa and the two look just alike. Dolly is stunned.

5) INT – SHAKESPEARE'S SONNETS' BOOK – DAY

She copies the sonnet from the book.

"MYSTERIOUS MUSIC" DISSOLVES

6) EXT – SHAKESPEARE – DAY

Shakespeare, dressed in black robe with a black and a white collar, speaks to DOLLY.

                    DOLLY
    The nun looked just like the Mona Lisa. Two rays of
    pure light, like sunshine were like golden, white
    threads to my eyes.

                  SHAKESPEARE
    Someday you will be one of them.
    Dolly looks puzzled and walks away.

RENAISSANCE FLASHBACK ENDS

MONTAGE ENDS

DOLLY'S FLASHBACK OF LINGERIE DEPARTMENT STORE

CAMERA MOVES IN on DOLLY'S head and CUT TO photo of a brain. SFX: multicolor swirls flash on the screen. BACK ON SCENE: CLOSE UP of a calendar that turns backward to September 18, 2010. The eighteenth is circled in red.

DISSOLVE TO:
INT - STORE, LINGERIE DEPARTMENT - DAY

SECOND NUN, 45, and the THIRD NUN, 40, dressed in the customary black and white apparel are seen shopping for underwear. They approach DOLLY who is with her sister, EMILY, 32, a friendly, heavy set woman who is a couple inches taller than DOLLY. In asking her for advice, Second Nun makes a comment to DOLLY about being one of us which upsets Emily. As a result, JJ, 17, a tall, slender teenager who is with them decides to search for the Nuns and maintains that they vanish into the thin air right before him.

PULL BACK to show the two nuns, DOLLY, her sister, and nephew.

SECOND NUN
(Laughs wildly)

MOVE IN to show the nun as she fingers white, black, pink, blue, and red under panties.

I don't know what color panties
I should buy our sister,

PULL BACK TO Third Nun.
THIRD NUN
(Blurts and looks at DOLLY)
Why don't you ask her?

MOVE IN, as the Second Nun approaches DOLLY who is with her sister, Emily and JJ, the nephew.

SECOND NUN
(Humoring the Third Nun)
What color panties should I buy my sister?

DOLLY
(Bewildered, shocked)
Pink.

SECOND NUN
(Grins)
You're one of us.
But you're not quite there yet.
I think I'll try white this time.

CAMERA FOLLOWS the Second and Third Nun as they walk away.
CAMERA RETURNS to Emily, JJ, and DOLLY.

EMILY
(Offended)
Why did she say you're one of us?
She never even spoke to me!

JJ
(Trying to comfort Emily)
You go to church three times a week.

EMILY
(Cocky)
Yeah, that's right. I go to church three times
a week. I'm a Christian, a Southern Baptist.
And how many times a week do you go to church?

DOLLY
(Baffled)
Once a week. On Sunday.

EMILY
(Still offended)
You're barely a Christian, and the nun spoke
to you, but not to me. I want to know why.

JJ
(Calculating)
Why don't we ask her? I'll find them!

DOLLY
(Looks around)
I don't see them anywhere.

EMILY
(Looks around and walks, talking)
Now where did they go? They have to be here.

JJ
(Determined)
I'll find them. They have to be in this store.

CAMERA MOVES TO DOLLY and Emily who look in disbelief.

DOLLY
(Firmly)
He's serious.

EMILY
(Contrite)
So am I!

CAMERA FOLLOWS JJ and shows <u>SFX</u>: The two nuns vanish right before his eyes.

TIME DISSOLVE

BACK ON SCENE. CAMERA MOVES to show JJ, DOLLY, and Emily.

>   JJ
>   (Mystified)
> They disappeared. They couldn't just walk out of
> store because I would have caught up with them.
> You're going to think I'm crazy. But I saw them.

>   EMILY
>   (Sharply)
> Where? You're not making sense.

>   JJ
>   (Still mystified)
> They vanished into thin air.

FLASHBACK OF LINGERIE STORE ENDS

CAMERA MOVES IN on DOLLY's head and CUT TO photo of a brain.

<u>SFX</u>: Multicolor swirls flash on the screen. CALENDAR SHOWS August 25, 2010, and the twenty-fifth is circled in red.

BACK ON SCENE:

DISSOLVE TO

INT - SCHOOL BUILDING - DAY

FLASHBACK BEGINS in the faculty room and shifts to various rooms of the school where each scene develops.

INT - FACULTY ROOM – DAY

DOLLY stands beside a copy machine with papers in her hand. She shows REVEREND HOLD pictures.

> DOLLY
> I have to have copies of these photos, but
> I don't know why.

> REVEREND HOLD
> Let me take a look.

CLOSE ON CUTS of photos.

QUICKCUTS
1) Shakespeare
2) Elizabeth I
3) Lord's Last Supper
4) Mona Lisa
5) Leonardo DeVinci as Older Man
6) Jesus as done by Leonardo Devinci

FADE IN. PULL BACK, the camera reveals Archangel Michael, wearing a blue robe. SFX: a soft blue light surrounds his entire body. Reverend Hold is not facing the angel, so only DOLLY can see him.

> VOICE OF ARCHANGEL MICHAEL
> You need to ask Reverend Hold about the postcard
> of the Mona Lisa.

CAMERA CLOSES IN on Reverend Hold and DOLLY.

> REVEREND HOLD
> (Shakes his head "no")
> I don't have one!

DOLLY
(Confidently)
Reverend Hold, the angel told me to ask you.

REVEREND HOLD
(Surprised)
Right! And Jesus talks to you too!

DOLLY
(Insistent)
You know where I can get a postcard of the
Mona Lisa, or you have one.

REVEREND HOLD
(Deep in thought)
Try Fifi, the French teacher.

DISSOLVE TO:
INT- FRENCH CLASSROOM – DAY

CAMERA MOVES TO the French teacher, FIFI, 60, an older woman
with brown hair who wears glasses and sits behind her Desk. DOLLY
stands in front of the desk insisting she give her the post card of the Mona
Lisa when she receives help from Archangel Michael who tells her what
she needs is in Fifi's pocketbook.

DOLLY
(Blurts out)
Reverend Hold says you have a postcard
of the Mona Lisa. I need it.

FIFI
(Blurts right back)
Ask him for his!

DOLLY
(Persistently)
I did! He said he didn't have one.
I was to ask you.

FIFI
(Matter of fact)
He does have one. I sent it to him from France.

DOLLY
(Pleading)
He won't give it to me.
I need yours.

FIFI
(Sick of the questioning)
I don't have any.

FADE IN of Archangel Michael in the blue robe.

SFX: A blue aura surrounds his entire body, as he appears behind FiFi.
BACK ON SCENE:

ARCHANGEL MICHAEL
(Whispers)
It's in her pocketbook.

MOVE IN on DOLLY, so Archangel Michael can walk away.

DOLLY
(Almost unable to speak)
The Mona Lisa is in your pocketbook.

PULL BACK on Fifi and DOLLY.

> FIFI
> (Mouthing the words slowly)
I have only one postcard.

> DOLLY
> (Desperate, trying to stay calm)
I won't keep it. All I want is to make
a photocopy.

CLOSE UP of Fifi getting into her pocketbook. PULL BACK to show her handing DOLLY the postcard.

DISSOLVE TO

INT - SOCIAL STUDIES CLASSROOM – DAY

DOLLY goes into Reverend Hold's classroom to show him the card and discuss the meaning of the postcard. While there, Reverend Hold shows her the photo of the Mona Lisa that Fifi sent to him from France while she was there on vacation.

> DOLLY
> (Demanding)
I need to see your postcard, Reverend.
Fifi says you have one.

> REVEREND HOLD
> (Grinning)
Here! Look what some jokester did.

CLOSE UP of the picture of the Mona Lisa holding a baby with a cord around its neck. PULL BACK on DOLLY and Reverend Hold.

48

DOLLY
(Concerned)
That looks like someone you know plans
to commit suicide.

REVEREND HOLD
(Suddenly surprised)
Like who?

DOLLY
(Thinking, speaking softly)
A younger person.

REVEREND HOLD
Let me see yours.

CLOSE UP of the picture of the Mona Lisa with a white cap on her head, two lips over the left area of the chest, and holding a chalice in her hands.

PULL BACK on DOLLY and Reverend Hold.

DOLLY
What do you think my picture means?

REVEREND HOLD
I know what it is. Someone over in France is
making fun of the Mona Lisa.

DOLLY
I can see that, but there's a meaning behind it
today. There's a reason for my having this card.

REVEREND HOLD
(Laughs)
Looks like a French cook using wine.

DOLLY
(Concerned)
Not to me. This one had me worried. (Pause)
It looks like someone I know may be having a
heart attack.

REVEREND HOLD
(Amused)
And the chalice?

DOLLY
(Determined)
That's a trophy.

REVEREND HOLD
(Giggles out loud)
I suppose you can see the engraving.
What letters are there? Jesus Christ.

DOLLY
(Serious)
No, G. W.

REVEREND HOLD
(Serious now, but puzzled)
I suppose the "G" could stand for God.
But I wouldn't know what the "W" means.

DISSOLVE TO:

INT - ENGLISH CLASSROOM – DAY

DOLLY is seen saying a prayer to God.

> DOLLY
> Dear God, if someone I know is having a heart
> attack, help the person. Help whoever it is go
> to the doctor, and get the proper treatment.
> Also, please God, make sure the Mona Lisa is holding
> the trophy.

DISSOLVE TO:

INT - FACULTY MEETING – DAY

CAMERA PANS AROUND THE ROOM catching TEACHERS' faces,
as MR.JACOB, the principal, 60, a tall man, partly bald with whitish gray
hair, entering goes to the front of the room.

DISSOLVE TO:

INT - RESTAURANT – DAY

CAMERA PANS a small group of teachers as they eat lunch.

DISSOLVE TO:

INT - OFFICE – DAY

DOLLY is standing in the office talking to the principal when the <u>sound
of the telephone ringing can be heard.</u>

CLOSE UP on the Mr. Jacob.

> MR. JACOB
> Hello. (Pause) She's right here.

                    (To DOLLY)
PULL BACK on DOLLY and Mr. Jacob.

                Mr. JACOB (CONT'D)
    It's for you. (Hands her the phone)

                    DOLLY
                (Into phone)
Yes. (Pause)
Dad's having an E K G.

                DOLLY (CONT'D)
An E K G is a normal part of a physical.
Sis, I don't know why you're worried. (Pause)
Look, you go to the hospital and check
if you want, too.
                (Pause) (Indignant)
Me? I have work to do here!
The kids are back in school tomorrow.
                (Pause) (Matter of fact)
Yes! We have Teachers' Meetings today, and
there's a bulletin board to do.
                (Pause)
If you find anything wrong, call me.

                DISSOLVE TO:
INT - ENGLISH CLASSROOM – DAY

CAMERA MOVES to DOLLY who is putting up a bulletin board when
ROY, 14, brunette hair teenager enters the room with JORDON, 60, an
older gray haired homely woman, having an introverted personality. God's
voice is heard and directs DOLLY to enroll this boy in her class. SFX:
A white light, representing, God appears over Roy's head. BACK ON
SCENE: CAMERA CLOSE UP of the light as God speaks.

GOD'S VOICE V. O.
(Filtered) (Hollow deep whisper)
This boy must be part of your English class.

PULL BACK to DOLLY and Roy.

DOLLY
(Looking heavenward toward light)
(Responds instantly to God)
(Looks at Roy and speaks)
I've been waiting for you.
We need to readjust your schedule.
You need to be part of my class.
(Walks toward the door)
Let's go to the guidance counselor.

CAMERA FOLLOWS DOLLY, Roy and Jordan who walk from the classroom, out the door, and shut it behind them.

DISSOLVE TO:
INT - GUIDANCE OFFICE – DAY

DOLLY, Roy, and Jordan are seen with JOHN NEWCOMER, 30, the guidance counselor, a distinguished looking business man, wearing a suit and tie. While convincing the guidance counselor to change the student's schedule, DOLLY remembers suddenly when she is a reading specialist in an elementary school. Roy tries to commit suicide by lying down in front of the school bus. Fortunately, the BUS DRIVER stops the bus just in time, and Roy is saved. Then, PRINCIPAL BROWN asks DOLLY to talk to Roy to determine why the boy wants to die. She is surprised by the answers. John Newcomer pulls her out of her day dreaming, and he changes the boy's schedule. Jordan is relieved the adjustments have been made. Because Jordon contributes DOLLY to saving Roy in the third grade, she is happy since this solution is what she desired and the very reason for coming to the school today.

>   DOLLY
>   (To John Newcomer)
> I need this young man to be part of my English
> class.

>   JOHN NEWCOMER
>   (Gently)
>   What's your name son?

CAMERA MOVES IN to show Roy and John only.

>   ROY
>   (Matter of fact)
>   Roy White. I'm an eighth grader.

>   JOHN NEWCOMER
>   (Wondering)
>   Are you in her class now?

>   ROY
>   (Firmly)
> No sir.

>   JOHN NEWCOMER
>   (Looking Roy straight in the eyes)
>   Roy, do you want to be in the class?

John looks through the schedules.

ROY
(Firmly)
Yes, sir. I'm an eighth grader.

JOHN NEWCOMER
You need seventh grade English, too.

DOLLY'S SUB-FLASHBACK IN ELEMENTARY SCHOOL

CAMERA CLOSE UP of DOLLY. CAMERA MOVES IN on DOLLY's head. INSERT: CUT TO photo of the brain. SFX: Multicolor swirls flash on screen. Neon lights show the date ....2005.

BACK ON SCENE:

MONTAGES:

1) EXT - SCHOOL BUS, ELEMENTARY SCHOOL - TRAVEL SHOT - DAY

A third grader, namely Roy White, 8, lies down along the sidewalk in front of the school bus, approaching the school to let students off for the school day. CAMERA PULLS BACK to show the school, Roy running, the school bus in motion, and THE CAMERA FOLLOWS the boy as he lies down.

MATCH TO:

MOVING SHOT of a school bus coming toward the boy. The bus stops short of hitting him.

2) INT - ELEMENTARY SCHOOL OFFICE - DAY

CAMERA MOVES in on a blonde haired man, PRINCIPAL BROWN, 28, thin, medium height, and rather nervous. DOLLY is wearing a much younger hair style. The principal asks her to pick up Roy and find out why he tries to commit suicide.

PRINCIPAL BROWN

See if you can find out why Roy tried to commit
suicide this morning.

DOLLY
(Softly)

Any ideas?

PRINCIPAL BROWN
(Matter of fact)

His father's getting a divorce. What else?
Who knows? Pick the boy up by himself. Then,
let me know what happens.

3)   INT - DOLLY'S READING CLASSROOM - DAY

This small room is the size of an office. One side of the room is lined with
shelves, showing elementary reading books on each shelf. A round table
with six chairs is in the center of the room. On the other side, there is
another round table equipped with reading games.

CAMERA MOVES IN on DOLLY who sits at a table with Roy, the third
grader. She has a reading book in her hand. Pencil and paper are on the
table.

DOLLY
(To Roy)

You feel badly today?

CLOSE UP of Roy who nods his head "yes".

DOLLY (CONT'D)
(Whispers gently)

What's wrong?

CLOSE UP of Roy who puckers his mouth, as if he's going to cry.

DOLLY (CONT'D) 2
(Softly)
You can tell me.

CLOSE UP of Roy shaking his head "no".

DOLLY (CONT'D) 3
(Sweetly)
Would you like to talk?

CLOSE UP of Roy shaking his head "yes".

PULL BACK to show DOLLY.

DOLLY (CONT'D) 4
(Puzzled look)
Then, why don't you tell me?

CLOSE UP of Roy who stammers.

ROY
(Faintly stammers)
I I I I can't.

CAMERA on Roy who has tears rolling down from his eyes now.

PULL BACK on DOLLY.

DOLLY
(With understanding)
You're in too much pain to talk.

MOVE IN as Roy shakes his head "yes". PULL BACK on Dolly.

DOLLY (CONT'D)
(Humoring him)
Can you write it?

Dolly (CONT'D)
(Urging)
Whenever I'm hurt, I write.
Then, I feel better.
(Pause, whispers)
Would you try to write it for me?

CLOSE UP as Roy writes. MOVE IN CLOSER AND FOCUS ON THE WORDS as he writes...

ROY
(Doesn't speak; writes)
I LOVE YOU.

PULL BACK to show Roy handing the paper to DOLLY.

DOLLY
(Smiles, says sweetly)
Roy, you are eight years old.
There is nothing wrong with loving someone.
It doesn't make any difference whether
you are eight or eighty. Loving someone is good.
(Pause)
Who told you loving someone was wrong?

ROY
(Barely audible)
My dad.

CAMERA RIDES on DOLLY and Roy.

DOLLY
I don't understand.

> ROY
> (Whimpering)

Dad's getting a divorce from Mom.

> DOLLY

I KNOW. (Pause) But why can't you love someone?

> ROY
> (Whispers slowly, stammers)
> (Trying not to cry)

Dad said not to love annyonnne.
Then, I woooouldn't get hurt.

CLOSE UP of tears running down Roy's face.

> ROY (CONT'D)
> (Whimpers)

But I caaan't help it.
I have these feelings.

PULL BACK on DOLLY and Roy.

> DOLLY
> (Smiling; reassuringly)

Good ones. Feelings of love are good.

> ROY
> (Shakes head no; he is troubled)

No. They're bad. (Pause) Dad says so. (Pause)

> ROY (CONT'D)

Now I'm bad. (Pause) I promised him.

DOLLY
(Whispers)
You promised him what?

ROY
(Continues to cry. Whimpers)
Not to looove…
(Pause)
annyonne.
I broke my prooomise.

DOLLY
I don't understand.

ROY
(Whimpers more)
(Sounds of whimpers heard)
The only way I can obey my dad is to kill myself.
No one will get hurt.

DOLLY
(Trying to comfort)
Love is not bad.
Love is good.
If you killed yourself, I would cry.
Your dad would cry. Everybody would cry.
Your dad loves you.
I love you.

ROY
(Puzzled)
But Dad said not to love anyone.

DOLLY
(Smiles with understanding)
I think your dad confused you.
I know your dad loves you.
Ask him tonight if he loves you.
I know he does.

DOLLY'S SUB-FLASHBACK ENDS

SFX: Multicolor streaks cover the screen. BACK ON SCENE: CAMERA
MOVES IN on DOLLY, and SFX: soft pastel shades streak out from
DOLLY's brain to reveal the daydream that has just happened in John
Newcomer's office. BACK ON SCENE: PULL BACK on John and
DOLLY.

JOHN NEWCOMER
(Pulling DOLLY out of the Daze)
Mrs. Day, where were you? I thought we lost you
for a moment. Where you in a daze?

DOLLY
(Disoriented)
I was.

JOHN NEWCOMER
(Jovial)
I've never had a teacher ask me to put a student
in her class when he all ready had one assigned. I
think you're crazy! This kid's an eighth grader, and
he even failed seventh grade English.

JOHN NEWCOMER (CONT'D)
I placed him in your Seventh Grade class, not the
Eighth Grade one.

> DOLLY
> (Beaming)
> I know I'm insane!
> But you wouldn't believe the reason,
> if I told you.

PULL BACK to reveal DOLLY, Jordan, John, and Roy.

> JORDON
> (Matter of fact)
> The reason we came to your room was to ask
> if Roy could be in your class. You saved
> him in the third grade, and he needs someone
> to save him again. Then, you told us, before
> we said anything.

> DOLLY
> (Looks heavenward)
> I know. I'll see you in class, Roy.
> Thank you, Mr. Newcomer.

> DISSOLVE TO

INT - ENGLISH CLASSROOM – DAY

DOLLY is in the classroom praying when John Newcomer enters with a message, letting her know her Dad is in the hospital because of a heart attack.

> DOLLY
> (Praying, looking heavenward)
> God, I just remembered the postcard.
> I do hope nothing is wrong with Dad,
> But if it is, please help him.
> And God, I don't know why you sent Roy here,

But help me help him too.

Amen

CAMERA MOVES to John Newcomer who arrives and enters the classroom.

JOHN NEWCOMER
(Seriously)
Were you talking to yourself?

PULL BACK on John and DOLLY.

DOLLY
Saying a prayer...

JOHN
(Worried)
That seems appropriate right now.

JOHN (CONT'D)
You need to get to the emergency room
at the hospital. Your sister called.
Your dad had a heart attack.

John leaves. CAMERA MOVES in on DOLLY in tears.

DOLLY
(Praying; tears in eyes)
Dear God, please help Dad live.

MATCH TO

CAMERA FOLLOWS DOLLY who is talking out loud and running down the hall to the principal's office.

DOLLY (CONT'D)

Help him until I get there. Make him well.

Please let that be a trophy in the Mona Lisa's hands.

DISSOLVE TO

INT - PRINCIPAL'S OFFICE – DAY

This scene is very brief, as DOLLY is talking to Mr. Jacob, the high school principal.

DOLLY

(Worried, partly breathless)

Dad's in the hospital.

He had a heart attack.

I have to leave. I'll call you.

MR. JACOB

Go ahead. I understand.

DISSOLVE TO

INT - WAITING ROOM – DAY

DOLLY is met by her sister, GLENDA, a younger, blonde hair lady who is slightly taller.

GLENDA

(With tears in her eyes)

The family is to be called to say their last
good byes. I've called everyone.

DOLLY

(Dazed)

Have you seen Dad?

GLENDA
(Sadly)
Yes, he's in the Intensive Care Unit.
Only one person from the family can go in
at a time. I came out to meet you.

DOLLY
May I go into see Dad?

GLENDA
Go ahead.

DISSOLVE TO
INT - INTENSIVE CARE UNIT – DAY

CAMERA MOVES to focus on Justin, and FAWNA, 60, a nurse, wearing a white net over gray hair under her nurse's cap. Justin complains of his feet until the nurse gives in to his pleading, and DOLLY comes into the room, trying to cheer Dad.

JUSTIN
(Chattering)
My feeeet are cooold.

FAWNA
(Sternly)
Socks are against the hospital rules.

JUSTIN
(Looks like he's been scolded)
(About to cry)
My feet are cooold.

FAWNA
(Switches to jovial personality)
Look what's in my purse.
A pair of socks that belong to my husband,
but he won't mind, if you have them.
I'm going to put socks on your feet because
God wants you to have them.

Fawna comes over and puts them on his feet.

JUSTIN
(Murmurs)
If God wants me to have them, I must be going
to get well.

FAWNA
(Assured; smiling; cheerful)
Yes, in time. Your feet will be warm shortly.

FAWNA (CONT'D)
But you better not tell the hospital on me.

JUSTIN
(Eyes widen; whispers back)
Not me, Fawna. (Smiles)

DOLLY approaches his bed. CAMERA MOVES in on the two of them.

DOLLY
(Cheerful)
You decided to come and find out what
hospitals do?

JUSTIN
(Meekly)

I guess so.

DOLLY
(Takes his arm)

You never were in a hospital before.

JUSTIN
(To DOLLY)

No.

CAMERA MOVES IN; DOLLY moves closer to Justin.

DOLLY
(Leans close; softens voice)

I've been in one five times. And they made me
well every time. (Pause) I'm sure God helped, too.
This place is good when you don't feel well.

(Looking sadder now)

I understand you have a pain in the heart.

JUSTIN
(Weakly, puckers to cry)

I did have. I'm just weak now.

DOLLY
(Confidently)

Then, this is a good place to be.

DOLLY (CONT'D)

The nurse and the doctor will take care of you.

JUSTIN
(Opens eyes wide)
Am I going to die?

CAMERA PULLS back on Fawna.

FAWNA
(Beams back)
No way. You have a warm heart and cold feet.
God wants you to have warm feet, too.
He's taking care of you.

DISSOLVE TO:
INT - HOSPITAL WAITING ROOM – DAY

CAMERA MOVES about the room, showing Justin's six children, four girls and two boys, along with SPOUSES, and SOME GRANDCHILDREN.

DISSOLVE TO:
INT - HOSPITAL INTENSIVE CARE UNIT – DAY

QUICK CUTS
1) INT - INTENSIVE CARE UNIT -DAY (TENS DAYS LATER)
A SERIES OF QUICKCUTS show a son or daughter at Justin's bedside,

MATCH TO

2) And then, the CAMERA MOVES in on an AMBULANCE TEAM, lifting Justin from the hospital bed to a transporting cot.

MATCH TO

3) EXT - AMBULANCE - TRAVEL SHOT - DAY

4) INT - AMBULANCE - TRAVEL SHOT - DAY

CAMERA CLOSE UP of Justin lying on the cot awake with an oxygen tank inside the ambulance.

5) EXT - GEORGE WASHINGTON HOSPITAL - DAY

6) INT - X-RAY LAB - NIGHT

Justin is given several tests and x-rays.

END QUICKCUTS

INT - GEORGE WASHINGTON HOSPITAL - PATIENT ROOM – DAY

CAMERA PANS around the room, and CLOSE UP of Justin, Tera, DOLLY, and Glenda. DR. WILLARD, 55, a distinguished, dark complexion gentleman, with Japanese features, wears glasses, and looks intellectual. DOT, 35, has short brunette hair, a shapely figure, reminding one of an aged Miss America. She is Tera's daughter.

CAMERA MOVES IN on Dr. Willard and Tera.

>   DR. WILLARD
>   (Matter of fact)
> You need a five way bypass on the heart.

>   DR. WILLARD (CONT'D)
> Our recovery rate here is ninety-five percent.

>   TERA
>   (Harsh whisper)
> And if he doesn't have surgery?

>   DR. WILLARD
>   (Firmly)
> He won't live over three months.

> **TERA**
> (Harshly; indignant)
No way.

> **DR. WILLARD**
> (Acts as if he doesn't hear)
What did you say?

CAMERA PULLS BACK on Tera, Dot, DOLLY, Glenda, Justin, and Dr. Willard.

> **TERA**
> (Severely)
Three months is long enough to live.
He can't have a heart operation.

> **DOT**
> (Cocky)
I agree with Mom.

> **DOLLY**
> (Concerned)
You have a ninety-five percent chance
of survival, Dad.

> **GLENDA**
> (Concerned)
You have to have the surgery.
You want to live. And we want you to live.

CLOSE UP of Tera and Dr. Willard.

TERA

(Arrogantly)

He can't have an operation.

I have cataract surgery tomorrow.

DR. WILLARD

(A last ditch attempt)

This operation needs to be done tomorrow.

He cannot live without heart surgery.

The cataract surgery can be done later.

TERA

(Angry)

No way!

DR. WILLARD

(Annoyed)

I would appreciate all of you stepping

into the hall. This decision involves

Justin's life. Not yours! He should make

this decision for himself.

CAMERA FOLLOWS Tera, Dot, Glenda, and DOLLY into the hall.

They look disgusted with one another. CAMERA FOLLOWS DOLLY down the hall. She walks away from the others. CLOSE UP, DOLLY looks upward to God.

DOLLY

(Prays)

God, are you there? If you hear me, God,

please make Dad say "yes" to the operation.

DISSOLVE TO:

INT - HOSPITAL ROOM – DAY

Dr. Willard, DOLLY, Tera, Glenda, and Dot are at Justin's bedside.

> DR. WILLARD
> (Firmly)
Justin has agreed to the operation.

CLOSE UP on DOLLY whose voice can be heard, but her lips don't move.

> DOLLY'S VOICE
Thank you, God.

PULL BACK to show everyone present.

> GLENDA
> (To Justin)
Good!

> DOLLY
> (To Justin)
Great!

> DR. WILLARD
> (Eyes shoot straight to DOLLY)
> (Then, eyes go to Glenda, sternly)
DOLLY and Glenda, I want you here for your dad tomorrow. You'll be here while Dad has surgery.

> TERA
> (Icy)
Dot's going to go with me while I have my cataract surgery tomorrow.

DR. WILLARD
(Sharply to Tera)
We shouldn't need you, Tera.

(Sternly to DOLLY and Glenda)
DOLLY and Glenda, be here at six sharp.
You can see your dad before surgery.

(To Justin)
Justin, you made a wise decision.
God and I will make you well.

DISSOLVE TO:

INT - WAITING ROOM – DAY

CAMERA FOCUSES on Glenda and DOLLY who are sitting on a sofa.
Across from them sit JASMINE, 65, and CALEB, 70.

JASMINE
(With interest)
What type of by-pass is your dad having?

DOLLY
Five ways…

GLENDA
(Innocently)
I never heard of anything but three ways.

JASMINE
(Matter of fact)
My son's only forty. He's getting an eleven
way by-pass right now.

DOLLY
(Stunned)
Wow! I mean that's a lot!

What did you do previously?

Jasmine is in deep thought, considering DOLLY's answer.

CALEB
(To DOLLY)
He worked for a post office.

GLENDA
(To Jasmine and Caleb)
I hope he'll be okay.

JASMINE
(Expectantly)
He will be.

DOLLY
(Meekly, not certain)
I wish I knew Dad would be okay.

JASMINE
(Assumingly)
He will be.

GLENDA
(Trying to remain cool and calm)
How do you know they'll be okay?

> JASMINE
> (Seductive type grin)
> I asked God, and He let me know.

> CALEB
> (Opens eyes widely)
> The *BIBLE* says that if two people ask for the
> same thing, God will grant their wishes and
> make the prayers come true.

> DOLLY
> (Forcing it delicately)
> But how can you be sure?

> JASMINE
> (Firmly)
> Caleb and I both asked God. He'll help 'em.
> Just wait!

FOCUS ON clock showing 8:00 o'clock. CLOSE UP of the clock.

> TIME DISSOLVE:

SFX: Hands roll to 6:00 o'clock in the evening.

BACK ON SCENE:

> DISSOLVE TO:

INT - RECOVERY ROOM – DAY

NURSE JESSICA, 25, a slender lady with red hair wears a white pants suit
uniform, and DOLLY are present. Justin is in bed.

CAMERA FOCUSES on all three of them.

> NURSE JESSICA
> He's fine. Just unconscious yet. Bet he's fine.

DOLLY
(whispers)
I've heard when someone's unconscious,
the person can still understand.

NURSE JESSICA
(unenthusiastic)
I've heard that. But no one knows for sure.

DOLLY
May I talk to him?

NURSE JESSICA
Yes. If he hears anything, the
monitor wilL show differences in the heart rate.

DOLLY
(Cheerfully)
Dad, you are out of the operation.
You are doing fine.

CLOSE UP of the heart monitor. PULL BACK to DOLLY.

DOLLY (CONT'D; REPEATS)
(Cheerfully, raises voice, softly)
Dad, you are out of the operation.
You are doing fine.

CLOSE UP of the heart monitor that moves downward.

PULL BACK to Nurse Jessica and DOLLY.

NURSE JESSICA
(Enthusiastic)
He hears you. He has relaxed.
This is exciting. Even though he's unconscious,
your voice relaxes his heart.

DISSOLVE TO:

INT - INTENSIVE CARE UNIT - HOSPITAL – DAY

Justin is lying in bed with Glenda and DOLLY at his bedside.

JUSTIN
(happily)
I'm glad that's over!

TIME DISSOLVE:

EXT - HOSPITAL - DAY (ONE WEEK LATER)

INSERT: CUT TO a sign,"ONE WEEK LATER". MOVE BACK TO
Justin in a wheel chair, being helped by DOLLY, Glenda, and Jessica. They
are putting Justin into the car.

DISSOLVE TO:

EXT - JUSTIN'S HOME –DAY

CAMERA MOVES to Justin getting out of the car while DOLLY and
Glenda help him into the house.

DISSOLVE TO:

INSERT: CUT OF picture of the Mona Lisa with a trophy in her hands.
CLOSE UP of a trophy. SXF: LETTERS SLOWLY APPEAR on the
trophy, "G. W".

BACK ON SCENE:

DISSOLVE TO:

INT - SOCIAL STUDIES CLASSROOM – DAY

CLOSE UP Reverend Hold. INSERT: picture CLOSE UP of the Mona Lisa, holding the baby with the cord wrapped around the baby's neck. BACK ON SCENE. PULL BACK on Reverend Hold and DOLLY who are discussing the recent happenings.

REVEREND HOLD
(Looks sad)
What you said came true.

DOLLY
(Puzzled)
I don't understand.

REVEREND HOLD
(Still sad)
My nephew committed suicide.

DOLLY
(Surprised)
When?

REVEREND HOLD
(Lowers voice; slower pace)
While your dad had heart surgery.....

DOLLY
(Stunned)
How?

REVEREND HOLD
(Embarrased; face reddens)
Rung his neck with a belt.(Makes a gesture with
his hand around his neck.)

DOLLY

I'm sorry.

REVEREND HOLD

I should have paid attention.

DOLLY
(Questions)
To your nephew?

REVEREND HOLD
(Sadly)
He was in another state.
(Pause)
But if I'd listened.

DOLLY
(Concerned)
No one knew. Not me. Not you.

REVEREND HOLD
(Serious)
But we need to pay close attention
to little things.

DOLLY
(Agrees)
Yes!

FLASHBACK ENDS

<u>SXF</u>: Multicolor colors swirl on the screen. BACK ON SCENE: CLOSE UP on DOLLY as colors come from her brain.

DISSOLVE TO:

INT - RESTAURANT – DAY

DOLLY is sitting in the restaurant, and this time she talks with CASEY, 35, a waitress, is extremely intelligent. Her job as a waitress seems as if she has been employed to solve the customers' problems, not just serve food.

CAMERA MOVES in on Casey and DOLLY.

> CASEY
> (To DOLLY)
> You seem to have a lot on your mind?

> DOLLY
> (Deep in thought, still evident)
> What would you say causes heart attacks?

> CASEY
> (Nonchalant, automatic)
> Eatin' the wrong food. That's what
> Mama always said.

> DOLLY
> Anything else?

> CASEY
> (Automatic)
> Lack of exercise. That happened
> to my Uncle Charlie.

INSERT: picture of a fat man eating. INSERT: picture of a fat man in a casket.

BACK ON SCENE. CLOSE UP of DOLLY.

>   DOLLY
>   (Looks at Casey's eyes)
> I always connected hearts to Valentine's Day!

PULL BACK AND CLOSE UP of Casey.

>   CASEY
>   (Sadly)
> Yeah, like when you're a kid in school,
> and don't get a Valentine.

INSERT: picture of children at school putting Valentines into decorated shoe boxes. INSERT: picture of one child opening a box and finding no Valentine.

BACK ON SCENE. PULL BACK to DOLLY and Casey.

>   DOLLY
>   (Prying)
> How would you feel?

>   CASEY
>   (Remembering; half broken hearted)
> Broken hearted. That happened to me
> in second grade. I got so mad!
> My heart started beatin', and I thought I was gonna
> have a heart attack.

DOLLY
(Matter of fact)
A lack of love could cause heart attacks.

CASEY
(Perky; regains composure)
Yeah! I'm glad I was only in second grade.

DOLLY
Why?

CASEY
(Thinking; serious expression)
If I'd been any older, I'd probably have committed
suicide. Love is pretty important. And the older
we are, the more emphasis we put on love.

INSERT: STOCK SHOT of sunset, ocean scene with two shadowed
figures walking along the beach.

BACK ON SCENE

DOLLY
(Rephrases words)
You are saying that heart attacks as well as
suicide can come from not feeling needed, and
others not showing love.

PULL BACK on DOLLY and Casey.

CASEY
Yeah! I think so.

                    DOLLY
We need to understand our past.

                    CASEY
                (Intellectually)
And the people who made us angry need
to be remembered.

                    DOLLY
                (To Casey)
We must forgive them for hurting us.

                    CASEY
                (Continued)
We can find comfort by sitting outside
and looking at nature.

INSERT: STOCK SHOT of nature.

BACK ON SCENE; CLOSE UP on DOLLY.

                    DOLLY
                (Understanding)
We need to become one with nature.

INSERT: STOCK SHOT of DOLLY sitting in Healing Garden in the
wooded area.

BACK ON SCENE: CLOSE UP of Casey.

                    CASEY
We need an Angel to touch us with love.
Any man could become my angel right now. (Laughs)

SXF: Raphael, a man as the Angel of Healing, appears beside the waitress. Pink auras surround him.

BACK ON SCENE: PULL BACK to DOLLY.

>   DOLLY
> We need to feel God's love.

SXF: White light shines into the room. PULL BACK to reveal Raphael, Casey, the White Light who represents God, and DOLLY.

BACK ON SCENE

>   CASEY
> Yes, I think that the Indians spent time
> with nature and Spirit.

INSERT: STOCK SHOT of Indians and woods.

BACK ON SCENE:

>   DOLLY
> What does nature remind you of?

>   CASEY
>   (All-knowing)
> Indians. Water. Sun. Wind. Land on earth.

>   DOLLY
> That's good. Perhaps the visions
> of the Indians are good. They know
> about Spirits, Mother Earth, and Father Sky.

BACK ON SCENE:

CASEY
(Excited)
What Indians? Did you know that Indians were
all over this land? Like, right where
you're sittin'; like right-where you walk outside?

DOLLY
(Amazed)
When?

CASEY
A long time ago, Indians believed their ancestors
Spirits continued to live. What were
you sayin' about Indians?

DOLLY
(Delicately)
Maybe that's why I think about Indians.
The wind, sun, moisture, and earth makes
me think of them. Each of these elements
represents Spirit.

CASEY
Indians were in America in the beginnin' of time.
They understood Spirit. Every Indian had a job to do.
They knew Spirit was eternal.

DOLLY
We could learn a lot from our Indian brothers
and sisters. Every soul has a purpose.

CASEY
(Understanding)
To find love…

INSERT: photo of multiple men and women. INSERT: photo of smaller hearts covering the screen. INSERT: photo of one large red heart. BACK ON SCENE. CLOSE UP of DOLLY.

> DOLLY
> (Smiling)
> To give love.

INSERT: STOCK CLIP of a child giving a mom a dandelion, buttercup, violet, or another wild flower.

BACK ON SCENE: CLOSE UP of Casey.

> CASEY
> (Seductive grin)
> I hope I find a man to give me love soon.

INSERT: MOVING PHOTO STOCK SHOT of a man walking forward

> MATCH TO:

to the waitress, Casey.

BACK ON SCENE: PULL BACK on DOLLY and Casey.

> DOLLY
> (Reacts to waitress)
> God can help you find that man.

> CASEY
> (Uncertain)
> Maybe I should ask the Angels of God?

<u>SXF</u>: Four angels appear. Gabriel, white robe; Uriel, red robe; Michael, blue robe; and Raphael, pink robe, stand beside

Casey. <u>SXF</u>: Enhancing the angels are auras: white, Gabriel; red, Uriel; blue, Michael; and pink, Raphael.

<u>SXF</u>: White rays shine from a white shape representing God to the angels.

BACK ON SCENE: CAMERA PULLS BACK to reveal angels, God, Casey, and DOLLY. DOLLY sees the visions, but Casey is unaware of the others appearance.

> DOLLY
> (Expectantly)
> How can I help children discover God's love?

> CASEY
> (Energetic)
> Don't ask me! I'm still tryin' to find a lover
> for myself.

> DOLLY
> Ask God and His Angels to help you.
> Now whom do you think I should ask?

<u>SXF</u>: The Angels and God disappear before DOLLY can ask them anything. She is unaware that Casey never saw any of them.

BACK ON SCENE:

> CASEY
> Try the lady in the bookstore.
> She's smart and knows everything.

DISSOLVE TO:

EXT - RESTAURANT – DAY

MOVE IN on DOLLY who walks from the restaurant

MATCH TO:

EXT - BOOKSTORE – DAY

As DOLLY walks up on the porch, she opens the door of the bookstore and goes inside.

DISSOLVE TO:

INT - BOOKSTORE – DAY

Even though Sarah, the clerk, in the bookstore never seemed like the type of person to help DOLLY with answers to how she was to help others turn to God, she decided to follow the waitress' advice. After all, all the pieces to the puzzle were not resolved, and DOLLY would accept any help she could get.

CAMERA MOVES IN on Sarah who is behind the counter and shows DOLLY across the counter.

SARAH
(Perky)
Do you need to see a Reverend?

DOLLY
(Unsure)
God has this assignment for me.
I need to find out how I'm supposed to help
children come to God.

SARAH (CONT'D)
(Full of energy)
And show them God loves them?

> DOLLY
> (Upset)

I don't know why God is picking on me!
I still don't know how nor do I understand
what He has in mind. I think I'm doing
a great job teaching the children, and then,
God comes calling.

> (Pause)

Goodness knows that I'm not supposed to discuss God in a public classroom. Next, I receive a message about being a screenwriter. I'm supposed to help the children come to God. But I don't know how.

> SARAH
> (Comforting)

Maybe I can help. Tell me about some things
that have happened to you during the past
three years.

CAMERA CLOSE UP of DOLLY.

> DOLLY
> (Informing)

I went to Waikiki Beach, Hawaii, in a wheel chair.

INSERT: STOCK SHOT of Waikiki Beach, Hawaii.

BACK ON SCENE: CLOSE UP of Sarah.

> SARAH
> (With interest)

And you learned how to be humble.
You learned to love and to understand the
handicapped.

CLOSE UP of DOLLY.

> DOLLY
> (Enthusiastic)
> Yes. You can say that!

INSERT: a picture of DOLLY in a wheel chair, being lifted to a boat by the navy men.

BACK ON SCENE:

> DOLLY (CONT'D)
> Especially when I had to be lifted to go see the remains of the Arizona at Pearl Harbor.

PULL BACK on DOLLY and Sarah.

> SARAH
> Go on.

> DOLLY
> Another time I was in Sedona and saw the Indian ruins.

INSERT: a picture of Indian writings on the stone mountains in Sedona, Arizona.

BACK ON SCENE:

> SARAH
> (Concluding)
> Then, you learned about destruction when there isn't any love.

DOLLY

Yes, the Indians had to move to higher ground
to get away from their enemies. I experienced
a medicine circle on another tour.

INSERT: a picture of a medicine circle in Sedona, Arizona.

BACK ON SCENE:

SARAH

Water, air, sun, and earth are parts
of the medicine circle and can teach forgiveness,
so the Spirit can heal.

DOLLY

Yes, I learned about Indian Spirit.
My husband and I toured the Hopi Indian
Reservation.

INSERT: a picture of the Hopi Indian Reservation.

BACK ON SCENE:

SARAH

You understand that the elders wish to teach
children about Spirit.

DOLLY

While there, I felt the sun. A wind blew.
Suddenly, rain poured. There was cold. Snow
came down.

INSERT:
QUICK CUTS
1) Sun

2) Wind blowing hair, clothing of Indians and tour group

3) Rain coming down on Indian tour guide and International Group touring the reservation

4) Snow coming down on the group

BACK ON SCENE:

DOLLY (CONT'D)
What a sight! White covered the earth.
There I stood on top of that Stone Mountain,
yet I saw the sun gleaming on the green grass
at the bottom of the mountain on one side. On
the other side, sprinkles of rain glittered on
the grass while snow covered the ground
around me. The weather changes took place
in a matter a few minutes.

SARAH
(Leaning forward on the counter)
Did you eat on the reservation?

DOLLY
Lamb stew with fry bread, plus blue corn pica
bread…

SARAH
You experienced the love of the Indians.
Eating their food made you become one of them.
We are all equal in the eyes of God.

DOLLY
I bought a Kachino Doll made by a Hopi.
Two of them as a matter of fact.

One Kachino I bought from an elderly woman.

INSERT: picture of two Kachino dolls.

BACK ON SCENE:

> SARAH
> Indians give the Kachino to an infant when
> the baby is born. The doll represents Spirit.

INSERT: photo of Kachino Doll given at birth...

BACK ON SCENE:

> DOLLY
> Yes, I know. (Pause) To teach them about
> Hopi
> Hopi Spirit.

INSERT: picture of Hopi Indians.

BACK ON SCENE:

> SARAH
> (Advising)
> Likewise, you must teach children
> about God's Spirit. What else?

> DOLLY
> What do you mean what else?

> SARAH
> (Calmly)
> What else have you done?

CLOSE UP of DOLLY.

> DOLLY
>
> I visited the vortexes in Sedona, Arizona.

INSERT: picture of one scene where there is a vortex.

BACK ON SCENE: PULL BACK on Sarah and DOLLY.

> SARAH
>
> Did you feel anything?

> DOLLY
> (Energetic)
> Yes. Energy! Lots of energy!
> At the Church of the Holy Cross,
> my husband pointed out Virgin Mary and child.

INSERT: picture of Virgin Mary and the child in stone at Sedona, Arizona.

BACK ON SCENE.

> DOLLY (CONT'D)
> I felt the masculine energy at most
> of the vortexes. My husband experienced the
> feminine energy.

> SARAH
> (All-knowing)
> Did you know we are energy forces?
> Even objects are energy. Can you remember
> an object giving off energy?

                    DOLLY
Yes.

FLASHBACK

Multicolor swirls come from DOLLY's head. <u>INSERT:</u> Picture of a brain
and then, multicolor swirls light the whole screen. The <u>sound of light music</u>
is heard.

                    DISSOLVE TO:
INT - SANCTUARY AT EMMITSBURG, MD – DAY

DOLLY and SHELDON, 40's, her husband, meet with a CHARISMATIC
NUN, stern, much older charismatic lady in the lobby of the sanctuary.

                    DOLLY
                    (Serious)
I need to find the angel with wings.

                    CHARISMATIC NUN
                    (Amused)
For what?

                    DOLLY
                    (Desperately)
I need a picture of the angel.
The National Be An Angel Day will be celebrated
in August, and I need the picture to convey
the message to my friends.

CLOSE UP of the Charismatic Nun.

                    CHARISMATIC NUN
Mother Seton is out back.

CLOSE UP of DOLLY.

> DOLLY
> (Forcing it)
> Does she have wings?
> (Insistent)
> I know Angels don't have wings,
> but I need the one with wings.

PULL BACK on DOLLY and Charismatic Nun.

> CHARISMATIC NUN
> (Smiles)
> Mother Seton doesn't have wings,
> but she's an Angel.

> DOLLY
> (Persistent)
> I must not be looking for her then.
> Do you know where I should go?

> CHARISMATIC NUN
> (Firmly)
> Close your eyes.

> DOLLY
> (Surprised)
> What?

> CHARISMATIC NUN
> (Insistent)
> Close your eyes. Just do as I say.

CLOSE UP on DOLLY with eyes closed, and then, the CAMERA MOVES to a head to waist shot of Charismatic Nun.

> CHARISMATIC NUN (CONT'D)
> (Expectantly)

What color do you see?

> DOLLY
> (Uncertain)

White?

SXF: White color abstract blocks emerge with bronze gold in the center.
BACK ON SCENE:

> DOLLY (CONT'D)

Bronze?

BACK TO CLOSE UP on DOLLY with eyes opening now and the CAMERA MOVES to the nun with a head shot.

> CHARISMATIC NUN
> (To DOLLY)

Close your eyes again.

CLOSE UP on DOLLY with eyes closed again. PULL BACK to DOLLY and the Charismatic Nun.

> CHARISMATIC NUN (CONT'D)
> (Firmly)

Good! How many are there?

> DOLLY
> (Confused)

What do you mean how many are there?

CHARISMATIC NUN
(Giving directions)
Just count them.

CLOSE UP of DOLLY whose eyes are still closed, and who gets a surprised look on her face. <u>SXF</u>: Color effects of one white shape on each side of the bronze gold shape.

BACK ON SCENE: CLOSE UP on DOLLY.

DOLLY
(Surprised; smiles)
There are three!

CAMERA MOVES in on the Charismatic Nun who is smiling.

CHARISMATIC NUN
(Grinning)
Keep your eyes closed.
Which one's big and which one's little?

CLOSE UP of DOLLY with eyes closed.

<u>SXF</u>: Color effects on smaller white shapes to the left and to the right of the bronze gold.

BACK ON SCENE:

DOLLY
(Whispers softly)
The white ones are little,
And the big one is bronze or gold.

CLOSE UP of the Charismatic Nun.

CHARISMATIC NUN
(Smiling)
That's good.

PULL BACK to show DOLLY who looks amazed. MOVE IN closer on the Charismatic Nun.

CHARISMATIC NUN (CONT'D)
Now I know where you want to go.
But first, you must promise to look
at our Angel Mother Seton, located
over to the right side of this building.

CAMERA MOVES to DOLLY, Sheldon, her husband, and the

Charismatic Nun who are standing together.

DOLLY
(DOLLY nods her head yes;
(She hesitates; then speaks.)
I promise.

CHARISMATIC NUN
(With confidence)
You'll be going to the hill behind St. Mary's
College. Write down the directions.

DISSOLVE TO:
INT- PARK CAR SCENE – DAY

CAMERA MOVES to DOLLY and Sheldon who sit it the car, looking out the window at ELIZABETH SETON, a white statue of the nun who founded private education in America. Unfortunately, at this time, DOLLY nor Sheldon know the meaning of the statue and could care less.

DOLLY

There she is.

INSERT: picture of Elizabeth Seton who is totally white and is seen as a statue.

SHELDON

What did she do?

DOLLY

How do I know? I'm as puzzled as you are.

SHELDON

(Questioning)

Must be pretty important to Catholics?

Are you going to take a picture?

DOLLY

(Mystified)

No. I don't know her. I was sent here

to take a picture of the Angel with wings,

but I do wonder why the Nun thought she was

so important.

DISSOLVE TO:

EXT - NATIONAL SHRINE OF ST. MARY, EMMITSBURG, MD – DAY

Two white angels are shown, one on the corner of each entrance to the National Shrine of St. Mary, and a huge, gold bronze statue of the Virgin Mary stands in the background. DOLLY interacts with Sheldon and the VOICE OF THE VIRGIN MARY.

SHELDON
Which angel are you taking for the picture?

DOLLY
All of them… I'll make sure I get the right one.

MONTAGE:

1) DOLLY takes the picture of one angel.

2) DOLLY takes the picture of the second angel.

3) DOLLY takes the picture of the Virgin Mary.

MONTAGE ENDS:

CLOSE UP: DOLLY looks heavenward, as if to Virgin Mary.

DOLLY
I've heard you appeared to people before.

INSERT: picture of a gold huge statue of the Virgin Mary.

BACK ON SCENE:

V.O. VIRGIN MARY
You must come closer to me.

CAMERA MOVES to a close up of DOLLY and Sheldon.

DOLLY
(To Sheldon)
It seems like she's talking to me.
I know she's not appearing right now
in a visionary form.

SHELDON
(Mischievous grin)
She doesn't have to. She's right here.
What's she saying?

INSERT: picture of the gold statue of the Virgin Mary.

V.O. VIRGIN MARY
(Filtered)
You must come unto me.
And you must help others come unto me.

BACK ON SCENE: CAMERA MOVES to DOLLY and Sheldon.

DOLLY
(Amazed)
Yes, it seems like she's talking.

SHELDON
(To DOLLY)
I didn't hear anything!
What did she say?

DOLLY
(Ignores the question)
I feel her energy. She's like a ray of sunshine.

CLOSE UP of statue of the Virgin Mary. SXF: She is shown catching the rays from the sun.

BACK ON SCENE:

SHELDON
You have that right! The sun's rays shine on her, all right.

FLASHBACK ENDS

<u>SXF</u>: Multicolor swirls light up the screen. The <u>sounds of soft music</u> are heard. <u>INSERT</u>: photo of a brain with soft swirls of color coming from it. The multicolor swirls flow

MATCH TO:

from DOLLY's head, and the colored lights disappear.

BACK ON SCENE: CLOSE UP on DOLLY.

DOLLY
That happened three years ago.

PULL BACK on Sarah talking to DOLLY.

SARAH
Do you remember any other times you experienced these energy forces?

DOLLY
(Automatic)
Yes.

FLASHBACK

<u>SXF</u>: Multicolor swirls light up the screen. The <u>sounds of soft music</u> are heard. <u>INSERT</u>: photo of a brain with soft swirls of color coming from it. The multicolor swirls flow from DOLLY's head, and then, nothing is seen, except for the entire screen enriched with various pale shades and shapes.

BACK ON SCENE:

INT - CONFERENCE ROOM – DAY

CAMERA MOVES around to ATTENDEES who are seated in a circle. In the middle of the circle sits LOGAN, 50, a handsome, good looking man. The attendees sing, and KAITLYN, 30, responds giving account of the visionary images. PHILLIP, 45, adds information to DOLLY's encounter, as the group experiments with toning by singing the person's name in the middle of the circle. Images that come are called out.

> ATTENDEES
> (Singing)
> Looooogaan! Looooogaan! Loooooogaaan! Looooooogaan!

> KAITLYN
> (Mouthing each word)
> Climbing a mountain…… a white light…

> ATTENDEES
> (Singing)
> Looooogaan! Looooogaan! Loooooogaaan! Looooogaan!

CLOSE UP on DOLLY.

> DOLLY
> (Surprised)
> There's an orange ball in my lap.

CAMERA FADES into lap. SXF: An orange ball appears. Energy rays can be seen coming from the ball.

BACK ON SCENE:

> DOLLY (CONT'D)
> I feel the heat!

INSERT: STOCK PICTURE of the sun in the sky.

BACK ON SCENE: CLOSE UP on DOLLY.

DOLLY (CONT'D)2

Now there's a sun in the sky.

And there's a stream of water beside me.

DOLLY (CONT'D) 3

I can see a greenish hue. There's a blue sky.

INSERT: CAMERA MOVES TO A CUT of a picture of a green stream of water, and a blue sky is overhead.

BACK ON SCENE: CLOSE UP on DOLLY.

DOLLY (CONT'D) 4

(Deep in thought)

The sun fades. The water puts out the ball

of fire. There is grass. It's green grass.

The grass covers the ball of fire.

The QUICKCUTS INTERACT with DOLLY's voice.

QUICKCUTS

1) Sun fades.

2) Water puts out ball of fire.

3) Green grass covers ball of fire.

QUICKCUTS END

SXF: Laser lights beam shoots from the ceiling into DOLLY's head. CAMERA RIDES on these beams of lights.

BACK ON SCENE: CLOSE UP of DOLLY.

> DOLLY (CONT'D) 5
> (Screeching)
Something's happening! Energy! Energy!
God help me.

SXF: Laser lights beam shoot from DOLLY's stomach to Logan's stomach.
SXF: Silver cords with added blue, green, violet, and white laser lights can be seen horizontally flowing from DOLLY's stomach to Logan's. These electrically rays flash between the two. (Optional laser light special effects can be done at Brevard Junior College, Melbourne, Florida, on a low budget, if desired.)

BACK ON SCENE: CAMERA CLOSE-UP of DOLLY.

> DOLLY (CONT'D) 6
> (Looking heavenward)
Help me God!

CAMERA MOVES BACK to show the whole circle of attendees.

Several of the ladies and gentlemen are doing the Roman Catholic Sign for Father, Son, and Holy Ghost.

CAMERA FOCUSES on DOLLY and Philip, the leader of the group.

> DOLLY
> (Mortified)
What happened?

> PHILLIP
> (Smoothly)
We'll find out when we come back.
It's your turn to sit in the circle next.

PULL BACK TO show everyone seated in the circle.

PHILLIP (CONT'D)

Everyone needs to break for ten minutes.

DOLLY's up next.

FLASHBACK ENDS

<u>SXF</u>: Multicolor swirls are seen on the screen. <u>INSERT</u>: photo of a brain and colors flow from this brain. Multicolors flash on the screen again, and the colors

MATCH TO:

connect to DOLLY's head.

BACK ON SCENE: CAMERA SHOWS DOLLY and Sarah talking.

DOLLY

(To Sarah)

I was so scared after feeling that ball of
energy and what took place! I left the
conference before I found out the meaning
of anything.

SARAH

Were you frightened after you came home?

DOLLY

You better believe it.

I couldn't get over what was happening to me.

SARAH

So what did you do?

DOLLY

I went to see a Roman Catholic Father,
and he sent me to a Life In Spirit Group.

> SARAH
>
> Did that help?

<u>FLASHBACK</u>:

<u>SXF</u>: Multicolor swirls slowly come from DOLLY's head, and emerge to fill the screen. <u>INSERT</u>: photo of the brain. The <u>sound of soft music</u> is heard, and multicolor swirls fill the screen. BACK ON SCENE:

> DISSOLVE TO:

<u>MONTAGE</u>

1) Small group of people singing Christian folk songs, and Jerry is playing the guitar.

2) Small group of people seated, and one person is seen reading the BIBLE.

3) Small group of people are praying over DOLLY.

4) Small group of people are singing.

5) Small group of people are eating.

<u>MONTAGE ENDS</u>

<u>FLASHBACK ENDS</u>

<u>SXF</u>: Multicolor swirls slowly come from DOLLY's head, and emerge to fill the screen. <u>INSERT</u>: photo of the brain. The <u>sound of soft music</u> is heard, and multicolor swirls fill the screen. BACK ON SCENE: CLOSE UP of DOLLY.

> DOLLY
> (Mystified)
>
> I discovered the Baptism of the Holy Spirit.
> Once I read the book of ACTS, I knew what
> happened, except I didn't ask God for anything.
> (Pause)

DOLLY (CONT'D) 2

He came calling on me. Later, whenever the
group asked God to baptized me in the Holy Spirit,
I felt the energy force, but it wasn't the same as the
first time. I guess it was the same thing; I'm not
sure. I didn't want to tell them about the first
time because they said it only happened once. The
group felt good about helping me.

PULL BACK to Sarah and DOLLY.

SARAH
(Responds with calculated anticipation)
Why don't you come to the Crystal Temple with me?
I'm going on May 31st.

DOLLY
(With interest)
Where is it?

SARAH
Flagler Beach, Florida.

DOLLY
What time?

SARAH
10 O'clock, May thirtieth.

DOLLY
(Thinking; making a decision)
Okay. Let me have your phone number
in case something unforeseen comes up.
Otherwise, I'll meet you there.

                    SARAH
              (Without missing a beat)
Fine. I need yours too. There has to be seven
of us to go the Crystal Temple, and I have
to find the others yet.

                    DOLLY
What will happen there, or what will I see?

                    SARAH
              (Assuring)
You'll understand your past, present, and future.

                    TIME DISSOLVE:

<u>SXF</u>: TWO WEEKS LATER is spelled out across the screen in neon lights.
BACK ON SCENE:

INT – Chosen Church– DAY

DOLLY is kneeling with Sheldon inside a church. She talks to God, and
the Voice of God answers.

CAMERA MOVES IN on DOLLY kneeling with her husband. CLOSE
UP of DOLLY looking at the Virgin Mary in stein glass. CLOSE UP of
the Virgin Mary who appears to be returning the stares.
CLOSE UP of DOLLY.

                 O. C. DOLLY'S VOICE
              (Internally talking to Virgin Mary)
I know you appeared in my bedroom.
I even understand that you want me to help
the children come to you. But I still don't know

what exactly you want me to do. I paid out money.
I went to a Screenwriter's Workshop. Yes, Mother
Mary, I met producers and directors. I think
you want me to write a movie. What I don't
understand is how! (Pause) Even if I wrote
the film, there is no market for God's work.
        (Pause)
How can I tell people about healing and love?
All the market wants is sex and violence.
If you had sex with another human, the
movie producers would be interested. People tell
me that love and healing without sex doesn't sell.
I'm just one person! I'm not God! Why can't you
understand?

SXF: White amorphous form light appears floating downward. Rays come
from the white light. PULL BACK to show church,

DOLLY, Mary, and the light. Sheldon is kneeling; however, his eyes
remain closed, and he prays with no other concerns of the surrounding
happenings of the moment. CLOSE UP on the White Light.

                O.C.GOD'S VOICE
                (Filtered)
                (Hollow, deep throated tone)
I do understand. You must show parents about
love and healing. God's love is more important
than sex and violence.

BACK ON SCENE: MOVE IN on DOLLY who looks up at the light.

                DOLLY V.O.
                (Resisting)
Why don't you tell the famous producers?

MOVE IN on light.

> O. C. GOD'S VOICE
> (Hollow, deep throated tone)
> They won't listen. They're busy worrying
> about making money.

PULL BACK to show DOLLY and the light.

> DOLLY V.O.
> (Feeling inferior)
> I'm a nobody.

> O.C. GOD'S VOICE
> (With confidence and power)
> Everybody is a somebody in God's eyes.

> DOLLY V. O.
> (Still in denial; trying resistance)
> I still think you should call on somebody else,
> if you want this job done.

> O.C. GOD'S VOICE
> I called on you. This job is yours.

CLOSE UP of DOLLY who shakes her head in disbelief.

> DISSOLVE TO:
> MUSIC
> "A World Prayer"

INT - CHURCH - DAY

The ENTIRE BODY OF THE CHURCH and all PEOPLE are holding hands and singing "A World Prayer." CLOSE UP of people's faces (scans all cast members), and then, CLOSE UP of everyone holding hands, as the prayer is sung.

"A World Prayer" Cont.
THROUGH TO:

PEOPLE
(Singing)
Our God is known by many names in many lands.
(Words of the World Prayer are sung.)

INT - CHURCH WINDOW – DAY

CLOSE UP of the stein glass window (Optional: Any church of any denomination can be used. Photo may be used. There is a cross with a dove on the window.) This visual reminds DOLLY of an earlier experience in a jewelry store when she first bought the cross. She has a flashback, taking her to the scene in a jewelry store. This scene is matched to another one showing God talking to DOLLY and encouraging her to buy this cross which she does from a CLERK behind the counter. As this flashback ends, DOLLY is shown in the church listening and responding to the white phantom form and God's voice.

CAMERA SWITCHES to a close up of DOLLY who looks at the window. CLOSE UP moves to DOLLY's hand. CLOSE UP shows a gold cross with a dove in her hand.

BACK ON SCENE:

MUSIC DISSOLVES
DISSOLVE TO:

FLASHBACK

CLOSE UP of DOLLY's head. <u>INSERT</u>: Photo of brain. <u>SFX</u>:
Multicolor swirls flash on the screen. CLOSE UP, calendar, 2000.

MATCH TO:
INT - JEWELRY DEPARTMENT STORE – DAY

DOLLY is looking at a cross the CLERK hands to her when God gives directions about why she must purchase this piece of jewelry. God talks to DOLLY internally; however, His voice is heard on the screen and His character is conveyed to the audience by a white form on the screen. Furthermore, DOLLY talks to God internally; on the other hand, Her internal voice is heard on screen with a varying softer sound, even though her lips do not move.

CAMERA MOVES IN when the clerk is removing the cross from under the glass. <u>SFX</u>: White phantom form light can be seen.

CLOSE UP, white light, and a voice is heard coming from the light.

> V.O. GOD'S VOICE
> (Filtered)
You must buy the cross.

BACK ON SCENE: CLOSE UP of the 14k GOLD CROSS WITH THE DOVE.

PULL BACK to DOLLY.

> DOLLY V.O.
> (To God; looks heavenward)
Why?

CLOSE UP of white phantom form.

> V.O. GOD'S VOICE
> ((Filtered)
You must join the church where you find this cross
in the window.

PULL BACK to show DOLLY and the clerk with white phantom form above them.

> DOLLY
> (To the clerk)
> I'll take this cross with the dove.

CLOSE UP of the clerk who rings up the purchase. She hands DOLLY the bag with the cross. CLOSE UP on DOLLY, as she removes the cross immediately and places it around her neck.

FLASHBACK ENDS

TIME DISSOLVE:

SXF: Multicolor swirls flash on the screen. CLOSE UP, calendar turns forward.

QUICKCUTS:

1) 2000

2) 2001

3) 2002

4) 2003

5) HOLD on 2004

SXF: White light can be seen with rays shining from it.

BACK ON SCENE:

> V.O. GOD'S VOICE
> (Hollow whisper)
> Trust in me.

CLOSE UP of stein glass window again. CAMERA MOVES to close up of DOLLY.

> V.O. DOLLY'S VOICE
> (Filtered; to God)
> Is this a sign from you, God?

CLOSE UP, white light.

> V.O. GOD'S VOICE
> (Firmly)
> I led you to this church. Listen to me.
> I'll show you the way to love and understanding.

PULL BACK to show DOLLY and white light.

> DISSOLVE TO:

EXT – CHOSEN CHURCH – DAY

CAMERA MOVES to FATHER and to DOLLY who comes out with her husband, Sheldon, and shakes his hand.

> DOLLY
> (Puzzled; holding out her cross)
> What's this cross mean?

> FATHER
> (Amused; grins)
> That's the Holy Spirit.
> (Gains composure)
> Why do you ask?

DOLLY
(Serious)
I saw the same cross on the left window in the church.

FATHER
(Warmly)
Yes! That's for the Holy Spirit.
The people wanted a window with a symbol
to represent God.

DISSOLVE TO:

MONTAGE

1   INT - DOLLY'S HOME - DAY

  A.   CLOSE UP of DOLLY sitting at the computer typing.

  B.   CLOSE UP of the computer screen.

  C.   CLOSE UP of WORDS.

FADE IN of an accident. The accident victim's soul leaves the body
and begins talking from the other side.

  D.   CLOSE UP of printer running off a treatment.

  E.   Papers are placed inside the envelop.

2)   INT- POST OFFICE - DAY

3)   EXT - POST OFFICE – DAY

V.O. GOD'S VOICE
(Warning)
I didn't direct you to write about an accident.
You didn't obey me.
You never wrote anything for me.

4)   INT - DOLLY'S HOME - COMPUTER ROOM – DAY

CLOSE UP, DOLLY is sitting at the computer when Archangel Michael, wearing a blue robe appears in the same room. <u>SXF</u>: Place blue aura around Michael.

BACK ON SCENE:

The <u>sound of Michael's voice</u> is heard, even though no lips move.

> V.O. ARCHANGEL MICHAEL'S VOICE
> Call Lee. He's at Johns Hopkins Hospital.
> He's been ill ever since his Mother died.

CAMERA CLOSE UP on DOLLY and FOLLOWS HER to the

> MATCH TO:

kitchen where she picks up the phone.

INTERCUT

INT - DOLLY'S HOME - KITCHEN – DAY

DOLLY calls Lee at Johns Hopkins Hospital.

INT - HOSPITAL ROOM – DAY

The <u>phone rings</u>, and Lee who is lying in the hospital bed talks to DOLLY.

INT - KITCHEN – DAY

CAMERA CLOSE UP, DOLLY dials the phone.

INT - HOSPITAL – DAY

The <u>phone rings</u>. CLOSE UP, LEE picks up the phone.

LEE
(Into phone)

Hello.

DOLLY

LEE, I called to see how Johns Hopkins
is treating you.

LEE
(Weakly but maintains humor)

DOLLY, I believe I'm about ready to join God.
The doctors here at Johns Hopkins don't know what to
do. I'm pretty sick. Maybe the first George Washington
and I can chop down a cherry tree.

DOLLY
(Humors him)

If you feel like chopping trees, no wonder
Johns Hopkins doctors are confused.

(Makes a decision)

Lee, do you believe in God?

LEE
(Unenthusiastic)

I used too, before I got sick.
Are you going to suggest I pray?

DOLLY
(Calmly)

I have this friend out in California.
Lee, he's a psychic healer.
Rich wrote a book on healing.

LEE
(Interested)
This friend of yours, what's he do?

DOLLY
He helps you pray to God.
Then, God makes the person well.

LEE
(Thinking)
I'd rather you help me pray.
Can you do that?

DOLLY
(Feeling incompetent)
My friend says I can, but I don't know how strong
my connections are. I don't know how this thing
works. I know that it works for Rich. He just says
this prayer to God, and whoever repeats his words gets
well.

LEE
(Agreeable, but disappointed)
I'll take Rich's phone number, but I don't know
if I'll use it.

DOLLY
(Softly)
I'll try praying with you. All you need to do is
repeat the words that I say.

LEE
Okay. Trying won't hurt.

DOLLY

Heavenly Father, you have taught us to love
unconditionally. Please surround Lee with your
healing light and help him to get out of the hospital.

LEE

Heavenly Father, you have taught us to love
unconditionally. Please surround me with your healing
light and help me get out of the hospital.

<u>SXF</u>: A white light begins at the top of Lee's head and is shown going
through the head, down through the throat, and flows through the chest
before going into the arms and hands. The white light continues through
the waist and down to the lower stomach area. Then, the light branches
into the legs and can be seen in each foot.

<u>INTERCUT ENDS</u>

DISSOLVE TO:

INT - DOLLY'S HOME - COMPUTER ROOM – DAY

CAMERA MOVES IN - DOLLY sits down at the computer and begins
typing a letter to the Angels of God. Three angels, namely, Gabriel,
Michael, and Raphael appear.

CLOSE UP on the words typed.

DOLLY
(Typing)
I need you, the Angels of God to help me.
Please help me write whatever you want.

CAMERA MOVES and PULLS BACK, Gabriel, Michael, and Raphael
appear behind DOLLY and look over her shoulders. *SXF: Gabriel, gets a*

white aura; Michael, the angel, has a blue one; and Rafael, the angel, receives a pink one.

BACK ON SCENE:

> DOLLY (CONT'D) 2
> (Looks up from typing; mystified)
> I feel like Angels are looking over my shoulders.

> DISSOLVE TO:

INT - LIVING ROOM – DAY

CLOSE UP of DOLLY reading the newspaper to Sheldon, as she decides to break from her writing. They are astounded by the appearance of the Virgin Mary in Clear Water, Florida. A NEWS REPORTER conveys the report on television.

> DOLLY
> (Trying to get Sheldon's attention)
> Just listen to this article in today's paper.

> SHELDON
> (Responds with interest)
> Which one?

CLOSE on DOLLY reading the newspaper. CLOSE UP on the WORDS showing them on a full screen, as DOLLY reads them aloud.

> DOLLY
> (Reading orally)
> Virgin Mary is making appearances in Clearwater,
> Florida. Thousands of people are flocking to see
> the image that has appeared on a building. Some
> believers have thrown fluid on the picture that

has appeared. In spite of these endeavors, the
Virgin Mary is still there, and the reporters of
newspapers throughout the world are writing about
the story.

Since the Virgin first appeared five months ago,
the news has subsided, but now, the story breaks
again.

PULL BACK CAMERA to Sheldon as he talks to DOLLY.

> SHELDON
> (Excited now)
> Do you think there's some hidden meaning?
> in the story for you?

> DOLLY
> (Shakes head no)
> Sheldon, I don't know of any.

> SHELDON
> (Interested in her thoughts)
> Do you think it's really the Virgin Mary?

CLOSE UP of a television set. CAMERA MOVES to a CLOSE UP of
the screen of the TV. VCR: the NEWS REPORTER announces. CLOSE
UP on the reporter.

> NEWS REPORTER
> (Matter of fact)
> Now, you can see what I saw on the glass.

CLOSER UP, VCR: INSERT CUT of the Virgin Mary again, and then,
CAMERA PANS TO DOLLY and Sheldon.

BACK ON SCENE:

> SHELDON
> (Surprised)
>
> What do you think?

> DOLLY
> (Confident)
>
> The image is certainly the Virgin Mary!

> SHELDON
> (Wanting more information)
>
> Who do you think put it there?

> DOLLY
> (Jovial)
>
> God! The Virgin Mary! Another human!
> Who knows? What I do know is that the
> image will make people think about the
> Blessed Mother.

> SHELDON
>
> Will you include that in the script?

> DOLLY
> (Still amazed)
>
> I don't know yet. Maybe the Angels will tell me.
> I don't even know if there's going to be a script.

> SHELDON
> (Grins)
>
> Maybe Virgin Mary will come to the Computer Room
> and talk to you.

DOLLY
(Humors him and agrees)
Maybe!

TIME DISSOLVE:

<u>SXF</u>: CLOSE UP, colors swirl. Calendar turns, May 31st.

BACK ON SCENE:

<u>MONTAGES</u>

1)   EXT - CAR - TRAVEL SHOT - DAY

CAMERA RIDES on DOLLY as she drives up the interstate and along the beach.

2)   EXT - CRYSTAL DOME, BEVERLY BEACH, FLORIDA - DAY

DISTANCE SHOT of the Crystal Dome, and CAMERA MOVES in on DOLLY getting out of the car. CAMERA FOLLOWS her. DOLLY joins BRITTANY, 24, and ALICIA, 22, who get out of another car. PULL BACK to show BILL, 25, BRANDON, 21, and RYAN, 31, get out of another car. HANNAH, 40, gets out of her car.

3)   EXT -CRYSTAL DOME - DAY

CLOSE UP of the door of the Crystal Dome, and SARAH who opens the door for them.

4)   INT - CRYSTAL DOME - DAY

CLOSE UP of the group being introduced to ZACK, a gray hair man in his 70's, the creator of the dome.

<u>MONTAGES END</u>

INT - CRYSTAL DOME – DAY

Sarah introduces Zack to the group. Another couple, a MAN, 60, and a WOMAN, 50's, have joined the group. Zack explains the purpose of the dome.

> SARAH
> (Serious)
> I want all of you to meet Zack, the creator
> of the dome.

CLOSE UP, they shake hands with Zack who is smiling. CAMERA MOVES in on the man in his 60's and the woman who is in her 50's that have joined the group. No formal introductions are made, as far as giving out any names. CLOSE UP of Zack.

> ZACK
> (With pride)
> This is where healing takes place.
> Some people discover their past.
> Others discover the present.
> Some of you will learn about your soul's
> purpose for the future. First, we need
> to go upstairs.

INT - SECOND LEVEL/CRYSTAL DOME – DAY

CAMERA FADES IN showing twenty-two chairs. Each person sits in a chair. DOLLY looks at the apparatus over the chair that is constructed of paper folded into a multidimensional pyramid. The same form is located under the chair.

CLOSE UP of Zack who hands DOLLY the same pyramid shape to cover her chest and stomach areas of the body.

ZACK
(Directs)
Cover your chest and stomach area with this.

CAMERA PANS the room to show different individuals with pyramids
over the stomach and chest area.

ZACK
(Informs, proud and all-knowing)
While sitting in the chair, healing takes place.
The chakras are opened as individual anchors.
We call on the Angels of God. Allow the Angels of God
to heal the mind, body, and soul. God, father, and
Holy Spirit give us higher energies. Allow us to
experience the Trinity. We know that people use only
ten percent of the brain now.
(Pause)
Open the chakras, so that ninety percent
of our brain cells are opened.
Balance each cell to the fullest.
                              Amen.
(Pause)

CLOSE UP of faces with eyes closed.

PULL BACK TO Zack and rest of attendees.

ZACK (CONT'D) 2
(Joyful)
When the process is completed, each one
of you will feel like a light body.
When you feel like you are light and airy,
come down stairs. Hold onto the rails
because using the legs again will require you
to follow instructions.

CLOSE UP of Zack getting out of his seat and standing.

                    ZACK (CONT'D) 3
I'll see you downstairs.

                    DISSOLVE TO:
INT - STAIRS/ CRYSTAL DOME – DAY

CLOSE UP of DOLLY coming down the stairs, and she talks of her feelings
to Zack. They are joined by Sarah who conveys the floating feeling.

                    DOLLY
                    (Baffled)
I feel like I'm floating, and I don't have legs.

                    ZACK
                    (Smiles)
Good!

MOVE IN on DOLLY and Zack.

                    DOLLY
                    (Grins)
This feeling is wonderful.
Just like I died and went to Heaven.

                    ZACK
                    (Opens eyes wide, smiles wider)
Yes, that's the feeling the soul gets when
one dies and goes to Heaven, I think!

                    DOLLY
                    (Overjoyed)
WOW! Going to Heaven won't be bad at all.

CLOSE UP, Sarah comes down the stairs.

> SARAH
> (Nervous)
> I'm floating. I can't walk.

PULL BACK to show Zack and DOLLY too.

> ZACK
> (To Sarah)
> Hold the railing.

INT - FIRST FLOOR/CRYSTAL DOME – DAY

CAMERA MOVES IN on DOLLY, Sarah, Alicia, Bill, Brittany, Brandon, Ryan, and Hannah. The elderly man and woman are together. CAMERA FOLLOWS Zack who leads them to two lone chairs with multidimensional pyramids and explains their purpose.

> ZACK
> (Informative teaching tone)
> Now that you've been upstairs, anyone of you
> may return at any time. Any of you may need
> to sit in a chair. This will open up the chakras.

> DOLLY
> (Curious)
> Can anyone use the chairs?

> ZACK
> (Instantaneously)
> Nope, only if you've been upstairs.

DOLLY
(Curious)
Can anyone go upstairs?

ZACK
(To DOLLY)
Only if seven or more people show up at a time
(Excited)
We're going back upstairs.
This time we'll experience Ascension.
You cannot go unless you've been healed.

CLOSE UP on the elderly man.

MAN
(Troubled)
I am terminally ill. I need more healing.

PULL BACK on Zack to show the man and him.

ZACK
(Softly)
Then, you'll need to go downstairs.

PULL BACK to show the elderly woman with the man and Zack.

WOMAN
(Concerned)
He's my husband. May I go with him?

ZACK
You don't need to.

                    WOMAN
                    (Determined)
I want to go with him.

                    ZACK
                    (Soft)
It's okay then. But you'll miss the Ascension.
You understand?

                    WOMAN
                    (Calmly)
Yes, I'll go with him.

CLOSE UP of another LADY who appears and leads the man and woman away from the group and downstairs.

INT - CRYSTAL ROOM/ CRYSTAL DOME – DAY

Zack takes DOLLY, Sarah, Hannah, Brittany, and Alicia upstairs to experience Ascension, explore the future, and determine how to help others. The four angels, namely Gabriel, Uriel, Michael, Raphael, and the Virgin Mary join the group to help guide them.

CLOSE UP on Zack.

                    ZACK
Each person will experience Ascension.
You will discover what can be done to help others.

CAMERA PANS the small room which is a pyramid structure lined with mirrors. A triangle ladder is in the center of the room. CLOSE UP of each rung, and on each one sits white crystals with a rose quartz in the center in vertical alignment with the others, sitting on four shelves. CLOSE UP of DOLLY, looking puzzled and frightened.

> DOLLY'S VOICE
> (Recalls the movie seen previously)
> This place reminds me of a time machine.

CAMERA MOVES TO Zack who closes the door.

> ZACK
> Yes, DOLLY. It's a type of time machine.

PULL BACK to reveal everyone in the room.

> ZACK (CONT'D)
> From this point, there will be no talking.
> Listen to the spirit. Allow the visions to come.

CLOSE UP of DOLLY and each one of the others - Alicia, Brittany, Hannah, and Sarah whose eyes are shut. CLOSE UP of DOLLY's face, opening eyes. Lips don't move.

> V.O. DOLLY'S VOICE
> (Frightened)
> I wonder what happened to Bill, Brandon, and Ryan.
> Did they chicken out? Is this thing built to summon God or the Devil?
> Is Zack the Devil in disguise?
> He did call the Angels of God.
> Perhaps I need to say a prayer of protection, just in case.

CLOSE UP as DOLLY closes her eyes.

> V.O. DOLLY'S VOICE
> (Prays; face points heavenward)
> Dear God, the Virgin Mary, and the
> Angels of God, I call on you for protection
> and for guidance today.

MONTAGE:

1) <u>SXF</u>: CAMERA MOVES to show Archangel Michael.

2) Raphael and Gabriel stand in the room behind the other ladies.

3) <u>SXF</u>: WHITE SPOT LIGHTS shine over the filtered bodies.

4) <u>SXF</u>: CAMERA MOVES TO show Virgin Mary, standing behind DOLLY.

5) <u>SXF</u>: White and Blue light rays soften Mary who looks as if she's filtered into the room.

<u>MONTAGE ENDS</u>

BACK ON SCENE:

CAMERA MOVES IN ON CLOSE UP of DOLLY's eyes. <u>SXF</u>: Multicolor lights swirl. CLOSE UP pages of a calendar turn.

CLOSE UP of WORDS ------

THE FUTURE

<u>INTERACT</u>

EXT - WHITE BACKGROUND/ PEOPLE/LADDER – DAY

CAMERA MOVES IN showing a white background. Only a huge ladder with seven rungs can be seen. LITTLE CHILDREN AND ADULTS appear on each rung. CLOSE UP of each group on each rung. <u>SXF</u>: AURAS CIRCLE the heads of each person.

<u>SXF</u>: RUNG ONE people have red auras.

RUNG TWO people have orange auras.

RUNG THREE people have yellow lights.

RUNG FOUR people have green lights.

RUNG FIVE people have blue lights.

RUNG SIX people have purple lights.
RUNG SEVEN people have white lights.

EXT - WHITE BACKGROUND/COLORED LIGHTS – NIGHT

CAMERA shows a ladder with seven rungs slanting upward.

<u>SXF</u>: A white aura surrounds the entire ladder.

RUNG ONE, a red light represents each person.
RUNG TWO, a orange light represents each person.
RUNG THREE, a yellow light represents each person.
RUNG FOUR, a green light represents each person.
RUNG FIVE, a blue light represents each person.
RUNG SIX, a purple light represents each person.
RUNG SEVEN, a white light represents each one.

EXT - WHITE BACKGROUND/PEOPLE/LADDER – DAY

CAMERA RETURNS to shot of people on the ladder with auras around heads as spelled out in first interact scene.

<u>SXF</u>: AURAS OF LIGHT develop and surround each entire body in appropriate colors.

<u>SXF</u>: EXT - WHITE BACKGROUND/ COLORED LIGHTS - DAY

CAMERA RETURNS to lights on the ladder scene. This time the ladder is surrounded by a white aura.

<u>SXF</u>: A huge white light shines from the left onto the colored lights on the ladder. CLOSE UP on the white light, God.

V.O. GOD'S VOICE
DOLLY, you must help people to become pure,
like the white lights. All people are like

little children. They can be innocent, show love,
and find happiness like little children.

SXF:

EXT - WHITE BACKGROUND/COLORED LIGHTS – NIGHT

QUICK CUTS

*1) Red lights move up one rung -
+2) Change to orange.
*3) Orange lights -
+4) Change to yellow.
*5) Yellow lights move to rung four -
+6) Change to green.
*7) Green lights move to rung five -
+8) Change to blue
*9) Blue lights move to rung six -
+10) Change to purple.
*11) Purple lights move to rung seven -
+12) Change to white.
*13) White lights step upward off the ladder -
+14) And float in the Heaven.

SXF:

EXT - WHITE BACKGROUND/PEOPLE - DAY

CAMERA RETURNS to people shot with auras surrounding their bodies
on the ladder. SXF: Green grass appears on the ground. The area above
the ground turns sky blue. CLOSE UP, people walk down the ladder and
touch the earth.

SXF: Soft multicolor lights whirl in circles, and then, form words. CLOSE
UP of the WORDS:

WORDS

EVERY SOUL HAS A PURPOSE.

"HARP MUSIC GOES FROM C, D, E, F, G"

<u>SXF</u>: All colors red, orange, yellow, green, blue, violet, and white swirl.

MUSIC DISSOLVES

BACK ON SCENE:

INT - CRYSTAL DOME – DAY

>   ZACK
> That's it!
> Did you get any insights into the future?

>   DOLLY
> Yes, I received the impression I'm to write
> a whole movie. God wants me to become a
> Screenwriter. I'm to teach the children
> about him, but I don't know if I'll get it
> on paper.

>   ZACK
> What do you think God wants you to write?

>   DOLLY
> All people regardless of age are Children of God.
> They are on different levels, and everyone is
> energy. The lower energy forces are red, and
> as the individual learns a lesson, the person
> changes his energy level to a higher level. Then,
> this is revealed by changing colors.

ZACK

That's good! What else?

DOLLY

It seemed as if these people transformed from
humans into light, and then, returned to human
form.

ZACK

Which would mean?

DOLLY

Life is eternal. People on earth can change their
Souls' purposes, just by learning new lessons.

ZACK

You said life is eternal. There must be more.

DOLLY

Yes, but this is really strange.

ZACK

Tell me anyway.

CLOSE UP of DOLLY and Zack.

DOLLY

God talked to me through an intrinsic force.
I could talk back to him without saying a word.
People on Earth could communicate with each
other intrinsically. Even the energy force of
the light waves seemed to be able to talk.
People who had passed over to the other side were
energy forms, and they communicated with

one another.

PULL BACK to show Sarah walking up to them.

                    ZACK
Some people have already reached this capability.

                    DOLLY
God wants me to tell others. But how can I find
away to satisfy his commands?

                    SARAH
You will. Come join us for lunch.

EXT - CRYSTAL DOME – DAY

CAMERA MOVES IN as Doris, DOLLY, Brittany, Alicia, and Hannah
get into one car.

SXF: All colors are shown. *INSERT*: *Photo of red flowers; next, photo of*
orange flowers; add photo of yellow flowers; follow with photo of greenery;
add photo of major blue flowers or scenery with blue color; add violet flowers
picture, and then, STOCK SHOT of all white scene.

BACK ON SCENE:

INT - DOLLY'S HOME / COMPUTER ROOM – DAY

DOLLY sits down at the computer to type. CAMERA MOVES IN
on DOLLY and the computer. CLOSE UP of DOLLY typing on the
computer keys. CLOSE UP OF COMPUTER SCREEN AND WORDS
on the screen.

DEAR GOD,

I have had lots of experiences that certainly are supernatural. Some of them I wouldn't believe myself if it hadn't happened to me. Throughout the past, I have argued with you and chosen not to believe you. In spite of this determination, you have persisted and shown me that I will have no peace until I share my experiences with you with the world.

SXF: Shades of red and orange lights swirl, and words appear in red and change to the color orange.

MUSIC in "C" Flat

INT - JEWELRY STORE - NIGHT

Two clerks in the jewelry store, NINA, 24, and SHELBY, 21, are anxiously waiting for customers when MARISSA, 80, wearing a long dress and a turban around her hair comes into buy a ring. Unfortunately, Melissa tricks Shelby and hides a diamond ring in her skirt.

QUICKCUTS
1) Nina, a clerk in a jewelry story, SXF: is surrounded by a yellow aura while Shelby, a clerk in the same store, is surrounded by a blue aura. Nina picks up the phone. Marissa, an elderly woman, SXF: surrounded by a red aura, comes into the store.

2) When Marissa tells Shelby she is dying of cancer and needs to sit down. Marissa tells her about a husband dying and leaving her lots of money, so she wants a big diamond before she dies. Shelby gives Marissa a chair, and she goes back to the counter.

3) Shelby gives Marissa a diamond ring.

4) Shelby takes the diamond back.

5) Shelby gives Marissa another diamond.

6) Nina talks to Shelby.

7) Marissa slips the ring into the pocket of her skirt.

8) Shelby and Nina talk.

9) Shelby gives Marissa another diamond.

10) Marissa returns the last diamond Shelby has handed her.

11) She walks out of the store.

12) Shelby puts the chair away.

13) Shelby looks at the glass counter.

14) CLOSE UP of the missing ring that isn't in the ring box.

15) Shelby goes to the phone.

16) CLOSE UP of the two policemen.

17) Shelby hands a picture of Marissa that she drew to the police.

QUICK CUTS END

MUSIC in "C" FLAT

INT - POLICE STATION – NIGHT

This brief scene shows Shelby at the computer drawing a picture of Marissa. The POLICE match drawn pictures of Melissa to a WANTED POSTER, prior to sending out her photo on a computer.

MONTAGE

1) Shelby is shown at the police station at a computer drawing a picture of Marissa.

2) Police match drawn picture to a WANTED POSTER. Merissa's photo the policemen have of Marissa is at a younger age

3) POSTER PICTURE is updated and NEW WANTED POSTER is sent out on the computer.

MONTAGE ENDS

MUSIC in "C" FLAT CONT'D

INT- LARSON'S JEWELRY STORE, HOUSTON, TX - NIGHT-

FIVE DAYS LATER
TIME DISSOLVE

Since DANIEL, 40, Manager of Larson's Jewelry Store, has seen the Wanted Poster, he recognizes Marissa when she tries to steal another diamond ring. He calls the police while ASHLEY, 30, a clerk in his store hands Marissa a ring and keeps her occupied until the police arrive.

QUICKCUTS

1) Marissa approaches Larson's Jewelry Store counter.

2) Daniel calls the police on the telephone.

3) ASHLEY hands Marissa a diamond ring.

4) Police arrive and handcuff Marissa.

QUICKCUTS END

MUSIC in "C" FLAT
THROUGH TO

INT - JAIL – DAY

In this scene Marissa is surrounded by a red aura because she has stolen diamonds. She is visited by DOLLY who is wearing a black suit with a white collar, showing she is portraying the role of a minister. SXF: A white aura surrounds the DOLLY. When Marissa prays and seeks forgiveness, the red aura surrounding her turns orange.

QUICKCUTS

1) Marissa sits behind bars. DOLLY, dressed as a minister, sits across from her. A *BIBLE* is on the table open. DOLLY points to verses. Marissa looks interested and appears to be reading.

2) DOLLY and Marissa kneel down at the chair to pray. <u>SXF:</u> DOLLY has a white aura surrounding her head. Marissa's red aura shines brightly.

3) DOLLY is shown leaving the jail, and Marissa is still on her knees.

QUICKCUTS END

DISSOLVE TO:
MUSIC in "D"

CLOSE UP CAMERA RETURNS TO Marissa. <u>SXF</u>: Red light surrounding Marissa's head changes to orange, as she continues to praying and looks Heavenward.

MARISSA

Thank you, God for your forgiveness.

MUSIC in "D"

INT - HOTEL - NIGHT

JANE, a guest relations representative at the hotel, finds her life is missing something, and DOLLY helps her discover a way of providing service to others, as a means to becoming more fulfilled.

<u>SXF</u>: Orange and yellow lights swirl, and then, the word

HOTEL written in neon orange lights changes to yellow.

Jasmine's shoulders to head area is surrounded by an orange aura.

BACK ON SCENE:

MUSIC DISSOLVE:

JANE

All I do is plan at this hotel and for what?

DOLLY

Money.

JANE

My life is missing something.
For a while I enjoyed helping businesses host
entertainment. Eating, drinking, and dancing were
fun. But now, I want more out of life.

DOLLY

Would you like to provide a service?

JANE

That's what I'm doing right now, but
no one appreciates me.

DOLLY

Have you considered helping the America Red Cross?

JANE

What I think I'd really like to do would be
to help get scholarships.

DOLLY

For whom?

                    JANE
Young people. Maybe I'd like to attend a business
college.

                    DOLLY
Go for it!

EXT - BUSINESS COLLEGE - Day

CAMERA SHOT of the outside of the building.

INT - OFFICE BUSINESS COLLEGE – DAY

CLOSE UP, Jane is sitting at a computer, and she helps a STUDENT, 18, in his twenties. SXF: An orange aura surrounds the student's head. SXF: An orange aura is over Jane. A yellow light approaches, surrounds Jane, and the orange aura is replaced by yellow. BACK ON SCENE: CLOSE UP of Jane's yellow aura, and the student whose aura is still orange changes to yellow, too.

                    MUSIC in "E"

SXF: Yellow and green colors swirl, and then, the words in two tones: yellow and green read,

        CHANGING FROM YELLOW TO GREEN

EXT - FOREST GREEN TREES / PARK BENCH – DAY

JARED, 30's, sits on one end of the park bench with DOLLY who rests at the opposite end. Jared is discussing his relationship with Kelly and whether to take a step toward more involvement. Kelly and Jared decide to quit spending lonely nights apart and become engaged to be married.

CLOSE UP of DOLLY and Jared. <u>SXF</u>: Surround Jared's head with a yellow aura. DOLLY's aura is white.

BACK ON SCENE:

> JARED
> Kelly and I have been friends for a long time.
> I was attracted by the way she gave tender loving
> care to sick people.

> DOLLY
> Nurses certainly help ease the pain.

> JARED
> Kelly's a great dancer, too. I enjoy being around her.

<u>INSERT</u>: Picture of Kelly and Jared dancing. CLOSE UP, Shoulder shot of DOLLY.

> DOLLY
> Have you become more than friends?

PULL BACK to reveal DOLLY and Jared.

> JARED
> I don't know. We see each other every day.
> Like today, she's coming here after work.

> DOLLY
> I'll bet you have a full afternoon planned.

> JARED
> Yes, and evening, too. I don't even like to go home alone anymore.

                    DOLLY
Have you ever considered marriage?

INSERT: Picture of bride and groom.
CLOSE UP of Jared.

                    JARED
Yes, but I can't stand rejection.

INSERT: STOCK SHOT of bride running away from the groom.
PULL BACK ON DOLLY and Jared.

                    DOLLY
Sometimes taking a risk is good. Listen to your heart. I'll see you later.

                    JARED
You gave me something to think about. Thanks!

EXT - FOREST GREEN TREES – DAY

DISTANCE SHOT of KELLY, 30'S, and Jared. SXF: A yellow aura surrounds both of their heads. BACK ON SCENE: CAMERA MOVES IN as Jared approaches Kelly. CLOSE UP of Jared putting his arm around Kelly.

                    JARED
I was talking to DOLLY this afternoon,
and I told her how special you are.

                    KELLY
You did? You're special to me too.

JARED

You really think so?

KELLY

Of course, otherwise we wouldn't be meeting
every day.

JARED

I hate going home alone at night by myself.
Do you ever feel that way?

KELLY

Sometimes!

CLOSE UP, Jared reaches a small limb on a Mulberry Bush, breaks off a
smaller twig, and ties it around her finger.

JARED

I know this is kind of weird,
But this Mulberry Bush is a circle of love
Just like in Phyramus and Thisbe;
I've lost my heart, and I was wondering, if
you would marry me.

KELLY

Yes.

JARED

What?

KELLY

Yes.

JARED

Oh, thank you, God!

CLOSE UP, Jared and Kelly kiss.

MUSIC "E" Changes to "F"

SXF: CLOSE UP, A green light circles the couple's heads, and their yellow auras change to green. BACK ON SCENE: And as they break ----

JARED

I'll exchange the mulberry bush for a diamond tomorrow.

KELLY

What counts is that you love me.

JARED AND KELLY

Soon we'll be together in one home.

MUSIC "F" Range

SXF: Green lights swirl to blue, and the words spell out

CHANGING FROM GREEN TO BLUE

DISSOLVE:

INT - BAR / RESTAURANT – NIGHT

Dolly sits on one side of the booth. LEE, 40, sits on the other side of the booth. Drinks are on the table. DIANE, 20, a waitress brings the food. Lee tells DOLLY about his intentions to marry, but there is a conflict of religious beliefs. When the conflict is resolved, he marries GIGI in the

Greek Orthodox Church with both the Greek Orthodox Father and the
Father from a Roman Catholic Church conducting the wedding.

SXF: A green aura surrounds Lee while a white one surrounds DOLLY.

BACK ON SCENE:

>   LEE
>   (Looking into DOLLY's eyes)
> We've been friends a long time.
> I had to see you. I don't know how to tell you.

>   DOLLY
>   (Looking into Lee's eyes)
>   DOLLY (CONT'D)
> Lee, I'm married.

>   LEE
>   (Picking up his drink)
> Yes, I know. That may be the reason I needed
> to talk to you.

>   DOLLY
>   (Playing with her straw)
> Why?

>   LEE
>   (Takes a drink first)
> To let you know I'm marrying a free spirit.

>   DOLLY
>   (Stunned; regains composure)
> Great! You had me worried for a minute.

CLOSE UP, Diane, the waitress, brings the food. Diane hands

Lee a plate of food.

> LEE
>
> Thanks!

Diane places the plate on DOLLY's side of the counter.

> DOLLY
>
> Thank you!

CAMERA CLOSES IN on Dolly and Lee.

> LEE
>
> A bar may not be the right place to discuss this.

> DOLLY
>
> What?

> LEE
>
> We want a church wedding. And I'm being led
> by the Spirit, but I'm Greek Orthodox. Unfortunately,
> my free spirit is Roman Catholic.

> DOLLY
>
> I used to be Methodist, but recently, I
> decided to become a Roman Catholic.

> LEE
>
> Why?

CAMERA CLOSES IN on DOLLY who looks sincere.

> DOLLY
>
> I believe God led me to the Roman Catholic Faith.

PULL BACK on Lee.

> LEE
> What do they believe?

> DOLLY
> It's just that God sent me some nun to show me something. Or I went into a Roman Catholic Church, and I connected ---like a Spirit drawing me.

> DOLLY (CONT'D)
> (Pause)
> What does a Greek Orthodox believe?

CLOSE IN on Lee.

> LEE
> I don't know, but I intend to find out.
> Some people claim that the whole church was
> together, and they broke apart over which
> way Christ laid his head when he died.

PULL BACK ON both of them.

> DOLLY
> That's hard to believe. I know Roman Catholics make the sign of the cross this way.

DOLLY demonstrates going from the forehead, to the heart on the left, and then, to the right.

> LEE
> A Greek Orthodox makes the sign of the cross
> this way.

Lee demonstrates going from the forehead, to the right, and then, to the left.

> LEE (CONT'D)
> But that doesn't help.

> LEE (CONT'D) 2
> Do I have a Greek Orthodox Wedding, or do we have a Roman Catholic Wedding?

> DOLLY
> This question is one everyone must answer for himself.

CLOSE UP, Lee takes his glass, touches DOLLY's glass, and says,

> LEE
> Let's give a toast to God,
> and let Him decide what's right.

> DOLLY
> I wish there were only one religion.

> LEE
> At least we have someone on our side.
> There's only one Supreme Being.

SXF: Swirling effects of white and black, splashing with pink and blue cover the screen.

> ROMANTIC MUSIC BEGINS

INSERT:

QUICK CUTS

1) Picture EXT - GREEK ORTHODOX CHURCH - DAY

2) Picture INT - GREEK ORTHODOX CHURCH – DAY

   Lee and Gigi are getting married. A Greek Orthodox Father and a Roman Catholic Father are part of the photo.

3) Picture INT - CHURCH RECREATION HALL - DAY

   Meals are being eaten by the wedding party.

4) Picture INT - RECREATION HALL - DAY

   Dancing by the wedding party begins.

QUICK CUTS END

MUSIC DISSOVES

SXF: Swirling effects of white shades.

CHRISTIAN MUSIC

BACK ON SCENE:

INSERT:

MONTAGE

1) Picture EXT - OUR LADY OF HOPE ROMAN CATHOLIC CHURCH - DAY

2) Picture INT - OUR LADY OF HOPE ROMAN CATHOLIC CHURCH – NIGHT DOLLY is wearing an all white dress and white heels. Sheldon, wearing a white suit, is standing by her side as they are being taken into the Roman Catholic Church.

3) Picture INT - ROMAN CATHOLIC CHURCH - NIGHT DOLLY is kneeling. FATHER is blessing DOLLY, as she takes Saint Elizabeth Seton's name.

MONTAGE ENDS

MUSIC DISSOLVES

INT - PORTRAIT SHOT - DAY

MUSIC INF
CHANGES TO "G"

SXF: Sheldon walks along beside DOLLY. The two walk from the back of the set. Sheldon is surrounded by a green aura.

DOLLY still has a white one around her. Blue spot circling lights enter from the side. Sheldon's green aura turns blue.

MUSIC IN "G"

SXF: Blue lights swirl with violet and the words appear in two tones: blue and violet.

CHANGING FROM BLUE TO VIOLET

MUSIC DISSOLVES

INTERACT

EXT - DOWNTOWN CITY STREET – DAY

CLOSE UP, of a seventy-six year old man, ANDREW wears a shabby suit with undershirt. His gray hair reaches his shoulders, and he has a white beard. Andrew prays to God, and asks him for food. DOLLY is led by God to Andrew where they eat in a restaurant, and he tells her about his past adventures in the war and why he lost his teeth. Andrew reveals how he comes to Washington, D.C. to find his son's grave when he's robbed by teenagers. And yes, DOLLY buys him a bus ticket to go see his friend who was in the service with him.

ANDREW
God, I'm hungry. I need a meal.

MUSIC: *THE CRY OF THE POOR*

CAMERA RIDES ON the old man Andrew who walks along Main Street talking to God and looking Heavenward.

THE CRY OF THE POOR MUSIC CONT'D

EXT - SUBURBS - TRAVEL SHOT - DAY
CAMERA RIDES on DOLLY's car.

MUSIC DISSOLVES

INT - DOLLY'S CAR – DAY

DOLLY
(Talking out loud to God)
Am I losing my mind? Are you talking to me, God?

SXF: A white light is seen in the car beside her.

BACK ON SCENE:

V.O. GOD
(Filtered)
I'm talking to you. Go to a restaurant.

DOLLY
I'm not hungry.

V.O. GOD
(Filtered)
Go to a restaurant.

DOLLY

Okay, you want me to go to a restaurant.
Even if I wanted to go to a restaurant,
how would I know which one?

CLOSE UP on the light of God.

> V.O. GOD
> (Filtered)

I'll show you.

EXT - MAIN STREET, DOWNTOWN, FREDERICK, MD – DAY

INTERCUT:

CAMERA MOVES IN on Andrew.

> ANDREW

Have you forgotten about me God?
I fought wars for you and for America.
Don't desert me.

INSERT: V.C.R. clipping from MEMPHIS BELLE (the movie on video, if possible or another suitable scene) of airplane with air force men.

SXF: A white light shines above Andrew's head. BACK ON SCENE: CLOSE UP of the white light.

> V.O. GOD

I'll answer your prayers. Hang in there!

SXF: The white light vanishes. BACK ON SCENE: PULL BACK TO Andrew.

> ANDREW

It seems like you're talking to me, God.

INTERCUT:

<u>SXF</u>: The white light shines in DOLLY's car. BACK ON SCENE: CAMERA PULLS BACK to reveal DOLLY and the white light. CLOSE UP on the white light.

> V.O. GOD
> (Filtered)
I'll show you.

CLOSE UP of DOLLY.

> DOLLY
You better because there must be hundreds of restaurants in this county.

PULL BACK on the white light and DOLLY.

> V.O. GOD
> (Filtered)
Turn left.

CLOSE UP of DOLLY and the steering wheel and show her putting on the left turn signal.

> DOLLY
Okay, if you say so.

PULL BACK to show the white light and DOLLY.

> V.O. GOD
Turn right.

CLOSE UP, steering wheel with the turn signal being given.

PULL BACK on DOLLY.

> DOLLY
> I hope you know what you're doing.

> V.O. GOD
> I should. I'm God. Turn left. Go slowly.
> Now park.

> DOLLY
> Oh, no! Between two cars! You must be crazy!

INSERT: Picture of two horizontal parked cars at meters with barely enough space between them for one car.

> V.O. GOD
> I'll help you.

EXT - PARK CAR IN FRONT OF RESTAURANT – DAY

DOLLY is parked on Main Street where there are lots of stores for shopping, including a restaurant. Andrew approaches and declares he's hungry, so the two of them go toward the restaurant.

> DOLLY
> (Out loud, looks Heavenward)
> You picked a good spot. I'd rather go shopping.

SXF: A white light appears. BACK ON SCENE: CLOSE UP OF light of God.

> V.O. GOD

(Politely ordering, filtered)
You're going to a restaurant.

CLOSE UP of DOLLY looking up.

V.O. DOLLY
(Lips do not move)
Then, you'd better show me a reason
just as soon as I feed this parking meter.

CLOSE UP of Andrew.

ANDREW
Can you spare a couple dollars? I'm hungry.

PULL BACK on Andrew and DOLLY.

DOLLY
What did you say?

ANDREW
I haven't eaten in two days.
I need to go to a restaurant.

DOLLY
Repeat that!

ANDREW
I need to go to a restaurant.

V.O. DOLLY
You really out did yourself this time, God.
You picked out this bum to go to a restaurant
with me.

ANDREW

Did you hear me?

DOLLY

Yes, I heard. We're going to the restaurant
together.

DISSOLVE TO:

EXT - RESTAURANT – DAY

DOLLY and Andrew approach the restaurant together, but he pleads that
he cannot go inside. DOLLY insists, and Andrew obeys.

ANDREW

I can't go in here!

CAMERA MOVES IN as he shows his dirty hands to DOLLY.

DOLLY

Yes, you are! We're going together. You said
you were hungry.

INT - RESTAURANT – DAY

White table cloths cover the table of the restaurant and lighted white
candles are in the center of the table. DOLLY and Andrew are seated at
one table for two where he insists on ordering chicken and potatoes from
the WAITRESS. Andrew tells DOLLY why he came to Washington, D.
C. where two teenagers robbed him, how he lost his teeth in service, and
his plans for the immediate future.

CAMERA PANS the room where people are seated wearing suits and ties
while others wear dresses with jackets.

CLOSE UP on Andrew in a navy blue air force suit from the 40's and only a torn undershirt can be seen under the jacket.

ANDREW

No tomatoes please! Chicken and potatoes. And coffee to drink.

CAMERA FOLLOWS AS THE waitress walks away and returns to DOLLY and Andrew.

DOLLY

Would you like to wash your hands?

ANDREW

No way. Those people in here wouldn't understand
how I look. They don't know the story. I'm not
a bum. I have a certain amount of dignity. Would you like to hear
my story?

DOLLY

Yes.

ANDREW

I came to Washington, D.C. to find my son.
He was the first one killed in the Panama, and
the government buried him. But I couldn't find
the grave. Some teenagers robbed me of my money.
They took my shirt.

DOLLY

Why did you come here?

CLOSE UP of Andrew.

ANDREW

My wife and I used to live here.
My daughter died, and then, my wife.
Some people used to work for me here.
But they're all gone too.

DOLLY
That's terrible, Andrew.

ANDREW
Would you like to know how I lost my teeth?

DOLLY
Yes.

ANDREW
I fought for America during World War II.
I was the one who dropped the bomb.
The thing went off, and I lost my teeth.

INSERT: V.C.R. clipping of soldier in video dropping the bomb which knocks out teeth.

CAMERA CLOSE UP as Andrew cries, wiping tears away.

ANDREW (CONT'D)
I was in the Air Force. My buddies, seven of us,
made a pact to stick together. They could have let
me die, but they didn't.

DOLLY
Where are they now?

CAMERA MOVES IN on the waitress bringing in the food.

> ANDREW

Three of us were alive, the last I heard.

They made a movie about us.

Anyway I'm going to see one of the war buddies.

He'll take care of me.

EXT- BUS STATION – DAY

CAMERA MOVES IN showing DOLLY and Andrew approaching the bus station.

INT - BUS STATION – DAY

CAMERA MOVES IN on DOLLY buying a ticket from a TICKET AGENT. CLOSE UP, she hands the ticket to Andrew.

SXF: A blue light surrounds the head and shoulders of Andrew and white lights surround DOLLY. Violet lights move in toward them. The blue lights around Andrew become violet.

BACK ON SCENE:

> ANDREW

I asked God for food because I was hungry.

Instead, he sent me an Earth Angel. Now I have a

ticket too.

CLOSE UP of DOLLY who reaches out and gives Andrew a hug.

> ANDREW (CONT'D)

God answers prayers.

<u>SXF</u>: Violet lights surround Andrew. White lights replace the violet ones around him. Dolly and Andrew are seen with white lights surrounding both of their heads.

BACK ON SCENE:

> DOLLY
> Yes, God sent me.

Andrew reaches out and gives DOLLY a hug.

> ANDREW
> God sent me an Angel. God bless you.

> MUSIC IN "G"
> SWITCHES TO "A and B"

<u>SXF</u>: Blue lights swirl to violet and then to white on screen. BACK ON SCENE:

> MUSIC DISSOLVES

<u>SXF</u>: All colors white, violet, blue, green, yellow, orange, and red swirl on the screen.

BACK ON SCENE:

> TIME DISSOLVE

<u>SFX</u>: Neon lights show November, 2011 flash on the screen.

<u>SXF</u>: Various shades of white swirl on the screen, mixed with soft violets. BACK ON SCENE:

INT -MEDICAL CONFERENCE ROOM - DAY

Dr. DAKOTA, 50, a medical doctor and DR. ELIJAH, 55, another medical doctor are explaining to the medical profession attendees who are supposed to be physicians and nurses about research. DOLLY is curious, and considering herself a professional has chosen to attend, hoping she'll discover more answers. DOLLY is not prepared for her deceased MOTHER who appears to her as a white light and whose voice she hears. Also, other deceased love ones communicate including her GRANDMOTHER, ERIC, and GEORGE. Special lighting effects are called for as LIGHTS turn into HUMAN FORMS NAMELY THE CONFERENCE ATTENDEES. There happens to be Angel harp music and the human forms acquire wings that disappear. ANGELS appear and GOD AS YELLOWISH WHITE LAZER RAYS OF LIGHT shine from his eyes to the beings. God walks out of the laser light taking a human shape, and everyone dances.

CAMERA PANS the room. SXF: showing the conference attendees surrounded by different colors of auras. BACK ON SCENE

CLOSE UP of Dr. Dakota who stands on a slightly elevated stage at the front of the room.

> DR. DAKOTA
> Some people have explored pleasant memories
> in their past. Others of you have journeyed
> through difficult and unpleasant times.
> All of us in the medical field who are in this
> room need to understand our own soul,
> as well as our patients and others.

CLOSE UP of Dr. Elijah who stands beside Dr. Dakota.

> DR. ELIJAH
> We humans transform through different levels: red, orange, yellow, green, blue, violet, and finally, white. I understand that much. Am I

correct that each of us is electric? Can we communicate to others at great distance?

PULL BACK showing only Dr. Dakota and Dr. Elijah.

DR. DAKOTA

Yes, to both questions. The light body or our
soul comes to earth, and every soul has a
purpose.

CAMERA PANS the attendees, and then, MOVES IN on DOLLY.

DOLLY
(Speaks out loud)

We need to help others to show them how to become
more like God.

WIDE SHOT from DOLLY to Dr. Dakota.

DR. DAKOTA
(Looks straight at DOLLY)

In the future, there will be no heart attacks,
no suffering, no violence. Each of us have a responsibility to help one
another practice unconditional love.

Dr. Dakata CONT'D
(Pause)

To end this session, I want everyone to relax
and let your mind go.

The <u>sound of music about GOING TO HEAVEN (chosen by the director)</u>"
is heard. All lights have been dimmed.

CAMERA MOVES IN on DOLLY's head and <u>INSERT</u>: CUT TO photo of the brain. <u>SXF</u>: Multicolor lights swirl on the screen.

BACK ON SCENE:

GOING TO HEAVEN MUSIC CONT'D

<u>SXF</u>: LIGHT BODIES resemble a string of white lights move above the heads of the attendees in a clockwise fashion.

BACK ON SCENE: CAMERA FOLLOWS the lights.

GOING TO HEAVEN MUSIC CONT'D

<u>SXF</u>: One LIGHT BODY goes upward in the back of the conference room. BACK ON SCENE: PULL BACK to show whole scene of all the light bodies swirling in oval fashion with the one light body going upward. CLOSE UP on the one light as it travels upward. CLOSE UP of DOLLY. <u>SXF</u>: One LIGHT BODY comes from DOLLY's head and goes upward. BACK ON SCENE:

CAMERA DISTANCE SHOT showing <u>SXF</u>: circle of light bodies.

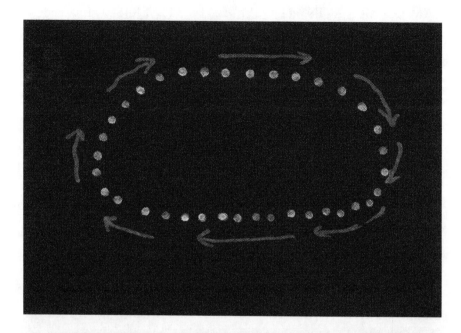

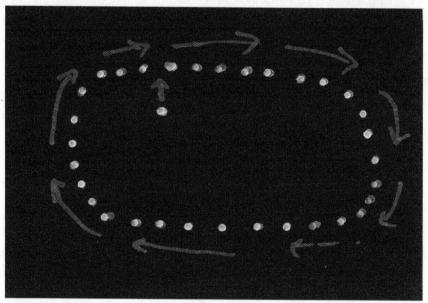

<u>SXF</u>: One light body from the back of the room has paired up with one other light body.

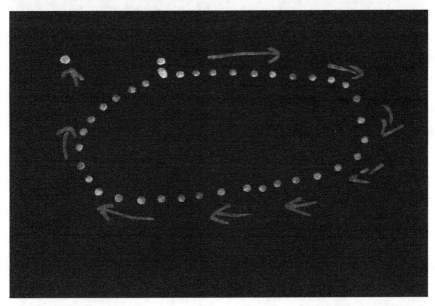

<u>SXF</u>: DOLLY's light body moves slightly above the circle and over to the far left of the conference center. <u>SXF</u>: FOUR LIGHT BODIES appear from the other side. They communicate with each other. MOTHER, GRANDMOTHER, GEORGE, ERIC, all look the same but DOLLY

can identify the voices. BACK ON SCENE: CLOSE UP of the four light bodies with a fifth light a few feet away from them, yet above the circle.

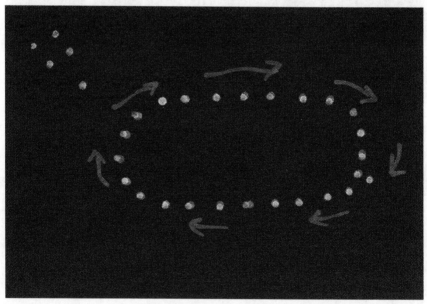

MUSIC DISSOLVES:

V.O. MOTHER
(Filtered)
I want to go to her.

V.O. GRANDMOTHER
(Filtered)
V.O. GRANDMOTHER CONT'D
You can't. She'll never go back.

V.O. MOTHER
I need to tell her about the curio.

V.O. GRANDMOTHER
You can't go to her. She heard what you said.

V.O. DOLLY
I recognize you. There's Mother, Grandmother,
George, and Eric.

V.O. GRANDMOTHER
Quick, Eric, take her back.

V.O. ERIC
I can't. It hasn't been long enough. George, you go.

CLOSE UP OF <u>SXF</u>: George's light body moves downward toward
DOLLY's light body, located just above the circle of other light bodies.
CLOSE UP of George's light body nudging DOLLY's light body.

CAMERA MOVES IN on the two light bodies of George and DOLLY
<u>SXF</u>: who are now adjacent to one another and have joined the others in
the circle which is still moving in a clockwise fashion. There are only two
double lights adjacent to each other in the circle. The rest are single.

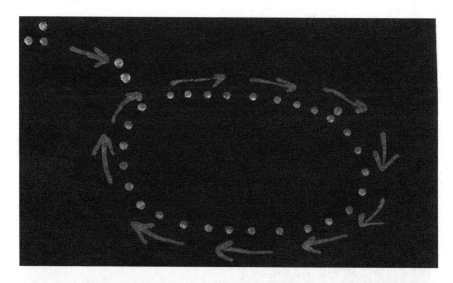

BACK ON SCENE:

CAMERA MOVES IN two lights that are paired, obviously DOLLY and George.

V.O. DOLLY'S VOICE
(Filtered)
I knew all of you.

V.O. GEORGE
(Filtered)
Yes. It's good seeing you again.

V.O. DOLLY'S VOICE
Why couldn't the others come too?

V.O. GEORGE
Shhhh. Don't talk. Time is too short.

V.O. DOLLY
This is heavenly. I never felt so good.

V.O. GEORGE
You must go back.

V.O. DOLLY
I just arrived.

V. O. GEORGE
You must go back. You have work to do on earth.

V.O. DOLLY
Like what?

V.O. GEORGE
Tell them about this experience. Go back now,
before it's too late.

V.O. DOLLY

Please don't make me!

GOING TO HEAVEN MUSIC BEGINS AGAIN

CLOSE UP, <u>SXF</u>: George's light body lines itself vertically with DOLLY, and hits hers downward out of the circle. CAMERA FOLLOWS AS <u>SXF</u>: DOLLY's light body makes a dive toward her human body and is seen entering her head.

"MUSIC CONT'D"

CAMERA ANGLE SHOT to show <u>SXF</u>: white light bodies floating around in darkness to the music, *Going Home.*

"MUSIC CONT'D"

<u>SXF</u>: LIGHTING DIRECTOR MOVES the white lights downward

MATCH TO:

and they look as if they entered the human bodies.

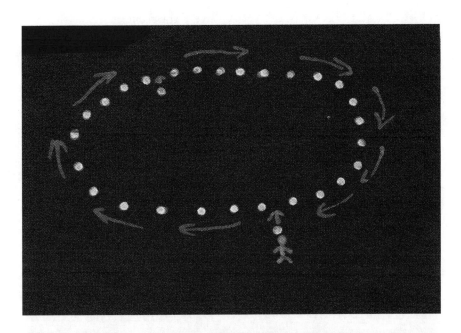

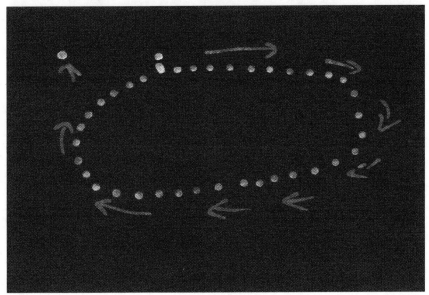

BACK ON SCENE: CAMERA RECORDS the scene.

DISSOLVE TO:

"MUSIC CONT'D"

INT - WHITE BACKGROUND – DAY

The LIGHTS turn into CONFERENCE ATTENDEES in human form, except they are wearing white robes trimmed in gold, and there are newly formed Angel wings on each one. The group dances to the original dance music, *GOD IS KING.* After special lighting effects, God can be recognized, and all the beings fall to their knees. The King namely God walks out of the light, takes a hand and dances. Everyone joins the dance as GOD IS KING is heard, or other dance music.

MUSIC CHANGES TO *GOING TO HEAVEN* MUSIC AGAIN.

SXF: LIGHTS have turned into HUMAN FORMS (CONFERENCE ATTENDEES). Each individual is wearing a white robe, trimmed in gold. Every person is seen with newly formed golden angel wings.

INSERT: White background with pearl covered ground, rolling White Mountains, and a river. SXF: Additional small white lights sparkle in the blue white sky.

GOING TO HEAVEN MUSIC DISSOLVES

SXF: Varying shades of white make a ripple, as horizontal stripes light the screen. BACK ON SCENE: The sound of Angel music with harps playing soft, floating, notes can be heard. CAMERA FOLLOWS to show the human forms with wings dancing.

DISSOLVE TO:

SXF: FADE IN, Wings disappear from the Angels who continue dancing.

MUSIC CHANGES TO
GOD IS KING

<u>SXF</u>: A circular shape with the colors yellow, green, blue, violet, and white rays swirl on the screen. <u>The sound of dance music of Director's choice or original, *GOD IS KING* is heard.</u>

<u>SFX</u>: The circular shape of color moves to the center of the screen. The Angels without wings in stark white robes trimmed in gold continue to dance. On the left and right of the screen is a stark white background.

<u>SXF</u>: A whiter light shines through the red, orange, yellow, green, blue, and violet rays. <u>SFX</u>: Laser lights develop the shape of a man in transparent white. <u>SXF</u>: Auras of yellow, green, blue, and violet lights outline his body.

<u>SFX</u>: Yellow laser rays of light shine from his eyes to the beings.

BACK ON SCENE: CAMERA FOCUSES IN, The beings fall to their knees, as they recognize God. <u>SFXL</u>: A halo of electric gold white light appears over each one's head.

MUSIC (CONT'D)
ORIGINAL *GOD IS KING* MUSIC

<u>SXF</u>: GOD walks out of the light. A Laser Light Form that looks like a human shape takes a hand of a human. They dance. <u>SXF</u>: God takes another hand and dances. BACK ON SCENE: CAMERA MOVES AROUND THE ROOM showing everyone joining the dancing as <u>the music continues.</u>

MUSIC CHANGES
"MUSIC IN 'B' "

SXF: Various shades of white swirl.

DISSOLVE TO
INT - CONFERENCE ROOM - DAY

DOLLY finds herself sitting in the conference room, hating to return from the experience she has just witnessed. DANIELLE 25, a slender brunette, stands in front of DOLLY crying and is waiting to see Mr. Dakota, the conference leader.

CAMERA MOVES IN to someone in the shadows who turns on the regular room lights. CLOSE UP of DOLLY with tears, streaming down her face.

CAMERA PANS on the Conference Attendees, as they begin to leave. CAMERA FOLLOWS Danielle who comes up to the front of the room in sobbing tears. PULL BACK to show Danielle, standing close to DOLLY, as she waits to see Mr. Dakota.

CAMERA MOVES IN CLOSER on Danielle and DOLLY.

DOLLY stands up.

DOLLY
Why are you crying?

DANIELLE
I became a light body.
I was talking to my grandmother,
And I didn't want to leave.

DOLLY
I know how you feel.

DANIELLE

You were the other light body who joined the
circle.

DOLLY

Yes, but they made me come back.

DANIELLE

Wouldn't it be wonderful to join them?

DOLLY

They contacted us. We didn't contact them.

DANIELLE

Give me your address. I don't want someone
to lock me up for being insane.

CLOSE UP of DOLLY opening her purse getting paper and pen. CLOSER
UP as she writes her name and address.

DOLLY

At least we'll have each other's company.
May I have your address, too?

CLOSE UP of DOLLY handing Danielle her address on one slip of paper.
In addition, she gives her a slip of blank paper and a pen. CLOSE UP as
Danielle writes her address, and she hands the slip to DOLLY.

DOLLY

By the way, what is a curio?

DANIELLE

A cabinet that shelves figurines... That's all I
know. Why do you ask?

> DOLLY

My mother wanted me to know about the curio she
sent or was sending. I don't understand.

CAMERA FOLLOWS as other attendees leave with the last one going
out the door. CLOSE UP on Danielle and DOLLY as they approach Dr.
Dakota.

DISSOLVE TO

INT - DOLLY'S HOME - DAY

DOLLY and Sheldon have returned home after the conference. They
discover some interesting mail.

CLOSE UP -A monthly calendar is shown. November can be read and
the year 2011. CAMERA FOLLOWS DOLLY and Sheldon, carrying
suitcases into the bedroom. Sheldon has letters in one hand. CLOSE UP,
Sheldon sits down one suitcase, and then, thumbs through the letters.

> SHELDON

Here's a special delivery. They tried to reach
you, but no one was home.

> DOLLY

I can't pick it up. I'm teaching.
Will you go to the post office tomorrow?

> SHELDON
> (Wondering if he should)

I guess so, if they'll give me your mail.

INT - DOLLY'S HOME / KITCHEN - DAY (MONDAY)

DOLLY is in the kitchen, and lays her school books on a side table. She goes to the sink and washes her hands and puts on an apron when Sheldon comes in and kisses her on the cheek.

CLOSE UP, Sheldon hands DOLLY the letter. CLOSE UP on DOLLY as she opens the letter.

> DOLLY
> (Excitedly)

It's from the local mall. I won a curio cabinet worth $500.
CLOSE UP on Sheldon.

> SHELDON

When did you take a chance on one?

PULL BACK on Sheldon and DOLLY.

> DOLLY
> (Matter of fact)

I didn't!

> SHELDON

Then, how did you win one?

> DOLLY
> (Puzzled)

I don't know. I wonder if that's what Mother meant that she wanted to tell me about the curio. I wonder if that's the one I drew three weeks ago that I wanted for our daughter.

CLOSE UP on Sheldon.

SHELDON

Fat chance. The one you drew doesn't exist.
There's no way. The one you want for our
daughter has beveled glass, stands five feet
high, and is light oak.

CLOSE UP on DOLLY.

DOLLY

I'll have to stop by the mall administration office tomorrow. Right
now, I don't have time to think about it.

DISSOLVE TO

INT - MALL OFFICE - DAY (Tuesday)

DOLLY is seen talking with THOMAS, 35, a tall slender man in a business
suit, who is the mall administrator. PHIL, 30, is his vice-president.

CAMERA MOVES IN on DOLLY, Thomas, and Phil.

THOMAS

Would you like to see what you won?

CLOSE IN, Phil removes a cover, and there is a curio cabinet, light oak,
five feet tall, four feet wide with beveled glass. CAMERA PULLS BACK
on DOLLY and Thomas.

DOLLY

(Gasps in surprise)
How did I win? I didn't take a chance.

THOMAS

Don't you want it?

DOLLY

Yes! I drew a picture of one. I wanted a curio,
just like this one for my daughter. But my
husband said it didn't exist.

PHIL

It does now, and it's all yours.

DOLLY

But how? I never saw this before in my life.

THOMAS

Neither did we. A man came through here this
past week and wanted to set up a display.
We told him, "No way" because he hadn't made
reservations in advance. But when he offered
us three curio cabinets for setting up his crafts,
we said, "Yes." Then, we decided to give them to
mall shoppers.

DOLLY

Why me?

THOMAS

After shopping in the mall, you showed your receipt and filled out a
chance on china set last month. You didn't win the china. We took
the left over names, and drew three of them. The other two winners
came by the mall first and chose the walnut ones which leaves you
with the light oak.

DOLLY

(To Thomas and Phil)
God answers prayers. This curio will be my
daughter's present.

PHIL
You need a truck. Do you have one?

DOLLY
No, however, I'll find a friend to help.

DISSOLVE TO:

<u>SXF</u>: These words appear on a full screen, as one electric light bulb begins with the first letter and continues to outline each letter.

HAPPINESS, LOVE, AND THE BELIEF IN GOD BRING JOY AND ETERNAL LIFE.

<u>SXF</u>: FULL SCREEN: One electric light bulb begins with the first letter and continues to outline each letter.

Words look like strung white lights.

YOU CAN BECOME A LIGHT BEING BY BELIEVING IN GOD AND LETTING HIM INTO YOUR HEART.

<u>SXF</u>: Two gigantic white lights in the form of hands appear beneath the words on the screen. Next, a lighted candle appears in the hands. Then, a green heart shape appears after the word heart, and the shape begins movement to indicate beating.

<u>SXF</u>: FULL SCREEN. CLOSE UP on the words in emerald green neon lights.

BY DOING UNEXPECTED ACTS OF KINDNESS, YOU CAN SPREAD LOVE INTO THE WORLD

BACK ON SCENE:

SOFT ROMANTIC MUSIC

<u>MONTAGES</u>

STOCK PICTURES are inserted.

1) Photo of someone giving another person flowers.

2) V.C.R. photos of giving someone cookies.

3) Photo showing a younger person driving an elderly person.

4) Photo of younger person carrying groceries for an elderly person.

5) a. V. C. R. photos of people getting ready to get on a boat cruise.

   b. A person falls down,

   c. and another individual willingly administers C.P.R.

6) Photo of someone fighting a fire.

7) Photo of a younger person shoveling snow.

8) Photo of an older person taking a group of younger people on a field trip.

9) a. V.C.R. photos showing lady making blankets,

   b. and then, taking the blankets to pass out to the homeless.

10) V.C.R. showing a person helping a blind person across the street.

11) a. V. C. R. showing people stacking food baskets,

   b. and then, making a delivery to a home where the packageis left at the door.

12) a. V. C. R. showing a person buying a gown in a department store,

   b. and wrapping the gown

   c. which is mailed to someone in another state.

13) a. V.C. R. showing one person crying.

   b. Another person calls the depressed individual.

   c. Then, the caller goes to the home.

d.   Next, ext, the two people are shown enjoying coffee and desert in a restaurant.

14) V. C. R. of a person writing a thank you letter to another individual telling how much the special person brought joy to the other one's life.

15) V. C. R. of a person in his/her early twenties raking leaves, and an elderly person watching and smiling.

16) Photo of younger person on the job with an older person.

17) Photo of younger person in a different type of job with an older person

18) a.   V. C. R. of an individual in a car picking up children

b.   and taking them to the beach.

19) a.   V. C. R. of a person sitting at a sewing machine,

b.   making clothes that are packed into a box.

c.   Photo shows box being mailed,

d.   and later, a college student opens the box,

e.   holds up the clothes,

f.   and hangs them in her closet

g.   that is almost empty.

20) Photo of baby clothes that are being given to a pregnant mother.

MONTAGES END

INT – DOLLY'S HOME/COMPUTER ROOM – January 2012

DOLLY is shown typing this script and SXF: the words of the twenty suggested ways of helping another person fill the screen.

BACK ON SCENE: PULL BACK ON DOLLY and the computer. SXF: Then, she types the words YOU ARE ELECTRIC into the script. The scene melts into the special effects of neon light.

<u>SXF</u>: Tubular double letters light up and moving liquid or electric neon lights flow through the tubes. Words fill the screen.

YOU ARE ELECTRIC

DISSOLVE TO
BACK ON SCENE

EXT - PARTY SCENE - DAY

The entire cast from the movie is seen having a party.

Balloons are in groups of colors. Each vertical balloon bouquet contains two red, two orange, two yellow, two green, two blue, two violets, and one white one at the very top.

<u>*SXF*</u>: *Neon lights in same colors as the balloons swirl through the letters.*

TRANSFORM YOUR HEART INTO A LIGHT BEING FOR GOD AND FOR LOVE.

MUSIC
HE'S GOT THE WHOLE WORLD IN HIS HANDS

The students step forward from the party scene and sing the song, ((Director may choose to use either the song *He's Got the Whole World in His Hands* or *We Can Make a Difference*))

CONTINUED

<u>SXF</u>:

1) A gigantic white heart is shown beating on the screen.

   Thumping can be seen.

2) Words appear on the heart, GOD'S HEART.

2) Numerous HEARTS form around the larger heart.

3) Smaller hearts thump to the music.

4) Smaller hearts appear to be dancing to the music

<u>SXF</u>: A huge LIGHT form appears on the left of the screen, white rays shine downward on the green grass. A blue ocean with rolling waves can be seen in the distance. <u>THE SOUND OF SINGING CAN BE HEARD.</u>

SOUND OF ORIGINAL MUSIC
SOUND OF ORIGINAL VOICES

When the light appears from above.
There may be more there than a dove.
Listen to the voice; you must obey,
For no one should tell God to go away.

You gotta take time to listen,
By spreadin' His love, people will glisten,
What God has to say is far more important,
Than makin' money, and sayin' I can't.

When the light appears from above,
There may be more there than a dove.
Listen to the voice; you must obey,
For no one should tell God to go away.

MUSIC ABOVE CHANGES

TO SOFT HARP MUSIC
SXF: A white background with pearl clouds appear in the blue and violet sky.

Words are written in neon lights across the screen.

First and foremost a special Thank You goes to God, for without this Supreme Being; these ideas would never have been possible. Certainly, Mother Mary and the Angels get additional thanks.

Another gigantic Thank You goes to Ester Luttrell, the world famous writer of TARZAN as well as THE MARY TYLERMOORE SHOW. Ester came to Orlando, Florida, to teach SCREENWRITING PARTNERS UNLIMITED in memory of her son who died in a car accident. This great lady advocates that violence can be changed into goodness. She is a guiding light in this world, and without her concepts and techniques in SCREENWRITING, this writer would not have been able to produce these results.

Paul Rabwin, producer of "THE X FILES" earns a special Thank You for his suggestions for adding the sketches of Special Effects. He states that for a Director to visualize what is not customary on the screen means that the writer must give added visuals to show how the new can become possible. Yes, Paul Rabwin, a workshop speaker at SCREENWRITING PARTNERS UNLIMITED must be remembered for the illustration of how lights can become characters and people by utilizing the proper effects in lightning.

Thank You

To Daytona State College faculty and learning specialists:
You get a big thank you for making this production possible.

Hilary Hemingway, granddaughter of the famous writer Ernest Hemingway, gets another Thank You because of her sponsoring the HEMINGWAY WRITER'S CONFERENCE held in Sanibel Island, Florida. During the sessions there, many magazine writers, book authors, and screenwriters expressed that the nature element that Ernest Hemingway's writing held dear were missing from current movies. Consequently, that element created by God was added to this script.

An additional Thank You goes to Rich Work and Ann Marie Groth Work, authors of the book *AWAKEN TO THE HEALER WITHIN.* Also, Rich Work is the author of *GOD THIS IS A GOOD BOOK!* and *PROCLAMATIONS OF THE SOUL.* This writer learned the power of positive energy and how to overcome the negative with positive love.

Without Jane Howard's book *COMMUNE WITH THE ANGELS,* and Jane's inspirations for the annual NATIONAL BE AN ANGEL DAY that took place in America every August for the past several years, this writer may not have paid attention to the necessary internal communications for this film. Thus, Jane Howard deserves a big Thank You, too.

SXF: DOLLY Day is seated at the computer typing, and these words appear in neon lights over the picture of her in the background.

Touching lives and teaching people the meaning of love through film, DOLLY consented to God's plan. She's hoping that others, too, will follow by becoming light beings and working for the Supreme Being. Then, heart attacks, violence, cancer, and other diseases will disappear from the world. *CREATING HEAVEN ON PLANET EARTH* is our responsibility and uniting together in unconditional love, we will experience peace, love, and joy. The answer is in the numbers, and you are the somebody who can make a difference.

About the Author

Nondis Lorine Campbell Chesnut is known under the pseudonym, Angel Love. She is the author of *A Touch of Love from Heaven*. Currently, she teaches at Daytona State College where this lady participates in the Humanities and Communication Department. Throughout her lifetime, she has been a screenwriter, author, consultant, reading, and language arts educator, learning specialist, and former President, Vice-President, Vice-President Elect, Secretary and Treasurer of the State of Maryland Reading Association. She has helped people from pre-school age to adults discover the magic of their own abilities to read, write, think, and succeed, so that they, too, can achieve peace, love, and joy. In doing so, she has appeared during television, radio programs, and even, in a movie. But the list doesn't end there, for Nondis has been a columnist for newspapers, an actress, a co-director of plays, and a conductor of workshops at the local, state, national, and international levels.

Her educational background includes completing writing courses from Charter Oak State College, the Institute of Children's Literature, and Screenwriters Unlimited. Nondis has credits for graduate courses from the Maryland State Department of Education, West Virginia University, Frostburg University, and Shepherd College.

With an A.G.S. in Reading from the University of Maryland, she implemented new programs in the elementary, middle, and high schools as a reading specialist. Her Masters Degree in Reading came from Shippensburg University, and her Bachelor of Science Degree with majors in English and speech was awarded to her by Concord University.

Having experience at Daytona State College, a public institution for all races, where visitors come from all over the universe, Nondis has a multicultural viewpoint, for she believes that we are equal and can develop our potential to create pure happiness by seizing the moment. In addition, she applies knowledge gained at Bethune-Cookman University, a private college known for not only training African-Americans but people throughout the world. Also, while an instructor at Hood College, a well-known girls' college that later, included men as well, Nondis learns that gender differences can empower the sexes. Her experiences in teaching are as vast as the ones in writing. She has taught pre-kindergarten, middle grades, and high school students in reading, writing, speech, debate, and English. Her expertise includes being a librarian, and teaching reading, plus writing to college freshmen and to post-graduate adults. Also, she has helped college students in content area subjects as a learning specialist.

This author's numerous awards included *Stanford's Who's Who Executive of the Year 2010-2011, Cambridge's VIP Award for Executives, Professionals, and Entrepreneurs 2009-2010, Who's Who in the World, Who's Who in America, Who's Who of American Women, Who's Who in Education, and Who's Who in the South.* Nondis received the President's Award from the State of Maryland Reading Association, the President's Award from the Washington County Reading Association, the Guidance Helping Award, Voice of Democracy VFW/Ladies' Auxiliary American Legion Heritage Writing Award from the Williamsport Lions Club, ASCD VFW Chairperson and Voice of Democracy Award, VFW Award from the Maryland District American Heritage Lions (Region II Lions Award), Williamsport American Heritage Lions Award, a drama award, and a citizenship award among others.

Nondis promotes discovering creative talents and utilizing them to create love, peace, and joy. She believes that each of us has an important job to do. We must love ourselves, love others, and create *Heaven on Planet Earth* through our own techniques and skills. Sharing a meal, giving a cookie that we baked, taking a photo, painting a picture, writing a letter, building a project, or babysitting are ways to make a difference in this world. She challenges each individual to take action.

Be happy. Help to change the world. Take the ideas from this book and implement them freely. Create your own movies, television programs, videos, and songs of love. Pick up a pen because as Shakespeare said that this instrument is" mightier than the sword." Use your words to create love and become an important piece of someone's heart today and forever.